Fancy Appliqué

12 lessons
to enhance your skills

Elly Sienkiewicz

C&T PUBLISHING

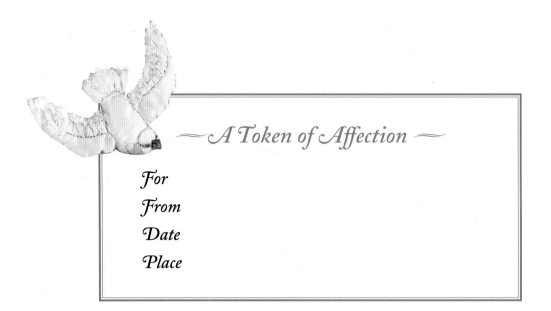

~A Token of Affection~

For

From

Date

Place

Copyright © 1999 Eleanor Patton Hamilton Sienkiewicz

Editor: Annie Nelson
Technical Editor: Joyce Engels Lytle
Copyeditor: Vera Tobin
Book Design: Ewa Gavrielov
Front Cover Design: Micaela Carr
Back Cover Design: Aliza Kahn
Graphic Illustrations: Alan McCorkle and Richard Sheppard ©1999 C&T Publishing, Inc.
Ink Drawings: Elly Sienkiewicz
Ink Drawings on pages 91-92: Norman Remer
Photography: Sharon Risedorph unless otherwise noted.
Front Cover Image: "Grackles and Grapes" by Elly Sienkiewicz, 1997, 13" x 13". The grape print of boughs and vines is Baltimore Beauties® fabric stitched in contemporary *broderie Perse*; the birds are fancy appliqué. The block interprets a classic Baltimore Album Quilt square, Pattern #81 from *Papercuts and Plenty*.
Back Cover Image: "Cameo Portrait: Moment of Wonder" by Elly Sienkiewicz

We take great care to ensure that the information included in this book is accurate and presented in good faith, but no warranty is provided nor results guaranteed. Since we have no control over the choice of materials or procedures used, neither the author nor C&T Publishing, Inc. shall have any liability to any person or entity with respect to any loss or damage caused directly or indirectly by the information contained in this book.

Library of Congress Cataloging-in Publication Data
    Fancy appliqué : 12 lessons to enhance your skills / Elly Sienkiewicz.
        p.   cm.
        Includes index.
        ISBN 1-57120-062-2 (pbk.)
        1. Appliqué—Patterns.   2. Album quilts.
    I. Title.
        TT779/S545   1999
        746/44'5—dc21   98-38812
                                                    CIP
The Copperplate Hand Alphabet on page 88 is reprinted from the *Zanerian Manual of Alphabets and Engrossing*, used with permission from Zaner-Bloser, Inc.

Trademarked (™) and Registered Trademarked (®) names are used throughout this book. Rather than use the symbols with every occurrence of a trademark and registered trademark name, we have only used the symbol the first time the product appears. We are using the names only in an editorial fashion and to the benefit of the owner, with no intention of infringement.

Published by C&T Publishing, Inc.
P.O. Box 1456
Lafayette, California 94549

Printed in Hong Kong
10 9 8 7 6 5 4 3 2 1

Table of Contents

Fancy Sampler Quilt I

Blocks by 1997 Appliqué Academy Challenge entrants and Elly
Sienkiewicz; quilt designed, pieced, and quilted by Lisa D. McCulley;
quilting design by Susan L. Connolly Clark, 54½" x 54½", 1997-1998.

Acknowledgments

Thank you, all who entered the first Elly Sienkiewicz Appliqué Academy block challenge and thereby inspired this book. Thank you at C&T Publishing, who have brought this work elegantly into print. Thank you to the folks at Starbucks and Barnes and Noble in Bethesda, Maryland, who provided me with a very "happening" office. Thank you to my precious friends and family who held true during this longest book write ever! And thank you, S., still the love of my lengthening life.

Grateful thanks to these 1999 sponsors of the Elly Sienkiewicz Appliqué Academy, my irrepressible fount of inspiration: Artemis Hand-dyed Silk Ribbons, C.M. Offray & Son, C&T Publishing, The Colonial Needle Co., Creative Import Designs, Inc. EZ Quilting by Wright's, Fairfield Processing, Quilt! Harris Publications, MKB/Mokuba Ribbon, P&B Textiles, PFAFF America, Quilter's Newsletter Magazine, Quiltsoft, Sakura of America, and YLI Corporation.

"A 'still life' in great art is a living thing. The objects are painted for what they suggest, and their presentation has no excuse if not to carry to the mind of the observer the fancy they aroused in the artist.…When a student comes before his model his first question should be: What is my highest pleasure in this? and then, "Why?."…This highest pleasure…[comes] to something like a just appreciation of the most important element of their subject, having eliminated its lesser qualities. The result is extract."

—Robert Henri, *The Art Spirit*, 1923

Dedication

Happy 84th Birthday
Eileen Mary Clare-Patton Hamilton Wigner, Mother.
The descriptive nomen, "lady," knows no more
courageous (or elegant!) exemplar. How fortunate am I,
still to call you Mummy.
And how fortunate is Little Ellie,
to call you Great Grandmummy.
Lucky are we can yet be with thee!

Of Stitches and Stones and Secret Gardens

My earliest memory is of a tiny world, bird's eye-viewed. Bird-like, I had plucked a bright berry from a hedge. My plump fist pulled that small red fruit to my lips. So great was my haste, that my mitten—a woolen flag clipped to my snowsuit—trembled. Whether the motion caught my mother's eye or whether the stolen morsel's taste made me spit that bitter fruit out, my next mind-shot remains a happy one: Multiple berries are pressed sweat-tight in my palm. Vividly, I recall the orb's pierced red skin, the golden meat squashed beneath it, the wooden pit within, as tiny as a bead.

Through memory's window, the wonder of that revelation still shines. Thus, a berried mystery (of bitterness and beauty) was threaded forever into the stuff of my life. When now I savor fancy threads, cloth, and beads, ribbons of recollection tumble into mind. These ribbons prove the secret all needle-workers know: the outward creation of stitched beauty brings to bloom an inward garden.

As for that tale of stolen fruit, I presume I was then on a walk with my mother. In a real sense, I still am. For my mother is an artist, and from her came my intrigue with small and lovely things: berries, wildflowers, and primordial stones plucked from the dust and stashed in a well-lined pocket. From her too, came that insistence to transform plain paper—or cloth—with the stuff of my journey, and from her came my pleasure in needle and thread. I am the middlemost of Eileen Mary Clare-Patton Hamilton Wigner's three children: daughter, daughter, son.

My sister, Erica, learned to read at age four. Naturally this pleased my grandmother, May Davina Ross Hamilton and her sister, my great aunt, Annie Ross. Both were schoolteachers (biology and French) and serious women. When we visited, Erica and I were both sat down to learn to read. Born just 18 months before me, Erica was tall, slim, and a bit shy. Her features were delicate: intelligent hazel-blue-gray eyes, softly changeable like the sky's storm-warning hues. Her skin was translucent, like a seashell in a watercolor. She bemoaned her ears, saying they stuck out. But to me they looked fragile and porcelain-like as they held back her sleek, straight hair. Her chin had character and seemed always to tilt upward, in strong-minded fashion.

I did not follow in my big sister's footsteps. Perhaps this is why I admire her so. By contrast, my mother reminds me, "You were always a difficult child; such a dickens!" Snapshots picture me coal-eyed, with a dark head of thickly irrepressible curls, short-cropped into a modicum of control; chubby, mischievous, thoughtful. When in the yard, I was harnessed to a leash that ran along the clothesline. I remember the joy when once I escaped and sat on my haunches in the street in front of our house. My mother notes that I laughed gleefully in my freedom. By means both physical and mysterious, we Hamilton sisters were kept within compass, and a good thing, that. But I did not early learn to read. Reluctantly, Grandma set aside the big-lettered book, and taught me instead how to thread a needle, knot the floss, and take magic-making stitches in brightly colored cotton. Like the piano lessons she funded so that I could play hymns, those stitching lessons were intended to equip me for something practical: darning, mending, and clothes-making.

Half a century later, I try hard to remember how and when I learned to stitch. What comes back is the absolute concentration: my world focused on the needle and on the thread that traced its path. The setting is forgotten—only the fascination of the needle's nip and pull are caught by that camera's eye. So the controlled became the controller and loved best those looped and locked embroidery stitches that bowed to her will: the French knot with the far-off name, the lazy daisy with the happy name, and the chain stitch which, like a crayon, could draw absolutely anything. Yes, I believe I learned to sew by learning embroidery stitches, like fabled American children of centuries gone by. Later, as a young mother, driven to find a secret garden all her own, I would add needlepoint's vocabulary to crewel's, and finally enter the community of quiltmaking, that most ennobling of all the grandmothers' flower gardens.

Now remembrance becomes understanding. My Scots grandmother's frugality must have seen literacy's second best in learned stitches, even those hoop-encircled and crowded onto a sampler cloth. Grandma was a woman of faith: she surely knew I would learn to read, albeit in my own time. Again, many years later, my daughter, Katya—dark eyed, thick haired, and magnetic—also frustrated the pre-school teacher who wanted her to read. Because the times were more intense, Katya was thoroughly "tested." With clear disapproval, her father and I were told, "Your daughter has all the necessary skills to read. But she is just not interested." I recalled my own childhood when, on Christmas, my sister and I got Toni® dolls: hers, a blonde, mine a hennaed brunette. Thereafter our dolls mirrored our interests: Erica's was always beautifully coifed, though clothed in a pinned washcloth sarong. In contrast, my doll's hair was macaroon-messy, but I stitched her such a wealth of clothes that I was rewarded with a doll's red-enameled wardrobe trunk on my next birthday. I loved that trunk so! One generation later, I was not worried when my young daughter had not yet learned to read: I knew, quite simply, that my Katya would blossom into someone more exceptional than the most highly quantifiable aspects of her promise.

When it suited her, Katya became a reader, as had I. For us both, childhood's stories opened up a world that often, like the needlework, was contemplative and inward-turned. I remember reading my mother's beautifully illustrated *The Secret Garden*. Just the concept of the tale—a place secluded, private, pretty—a secret place of one's own—says much to me about that world where a needle is our guide. Every needlewoman knows that stitching turns us inward to ourselves, or to far-off and other-worldly places. Sometimes it erases all conscious thought, so that the pleasure of the stitches' rhythm is paradise enough. So intimate is this private journey that we may be shy to share the fruit of our hand. But when, habitually, we show our needleart within an affirming circle, we come to know and to accept our own selves better. And so it is that in needleart many have found solace, affirmation, and self-acceptance.

In some mysterious way, quilts, to the late twentieth century quiltmaker, now frame a community that crosses barriers of age, sex, income, education, politics, or religion. With tenderness, quiltmakers protect each other and the sanctity of their circle. So cherished is quiltmaking's communal aspect, so rare has become such trust invested in so large a group, that we understand the term quiltmaker to mean more than simply someone who makes quilts. With this trust has come freedom of another sort: some guild members easily confess that they are more "communal quiltmakers" than quiltmakers in cloth. Others feel quite free to incorporate newly discovered crafts into their quilts, or simply to branch out for a while into related modes of needlework expression, and then return to quiltmaking. Thus nourished by an astonishing blend of freedom and trust, many now explore beading, pin-weaving, tatting, lace-making, embroidery, knitting, crocheting, calligraphy, dyeing, and ribbonwork—all within the quiltmakers' sheltered circle of like-minded friends.

So it is as a quiltmaker come back to first-learned embroidery and appliqué that I write this book on fancywork. But it is the quiltmaking that has enriched my adult life so. It is the quiltmaking which has opened up that secret garden of my mind and hands, to a world infinitely more beautiful for being a communal world. And Grandma Hamilton would be pleased. For her reluctant reader who loved to stitch now also loves to write about it, so much so that thereby you and I, dear reader, can sit sharingly in silence, each in secret gardens of our own, and stitch together.

Appliqué Plain and Fancy

Plain or fancy, piecing dominates American quilt-making, and its basics are easier to learn than are those of appliqué. Our folklore names appliqué "patchwork," bringing mending to mind. Yet most appliqué—ancient or modern—is wedded to fancy-work. While appliqué admits a wide variety of technical approaches, that very fact makes mastery a challenge. My *Appliqué 12 Easy Ways!* explores the how, when, and why of basic appliqué techniques. Since it was first published in 1991, our facility with appliqué has burgeoned.

This book instructs in the realm of fancy appliqué. As in a workbook, the 12 lessons teach consecutively; each builds on the one before. Every technique is taught on a quilt square whose pattern can be found in the Pattern Section. For block preparation, pattern transfer, and block completion, refer to page 110 in the Pattern Section. Basic materials are discussed on pages 12 to 22 in Setting Stitchery's Stage. Each lesson lists the materials needed, while help with hard-to-find supplies is located through Sources. Appliqué's non-decorative stitches and state-of-the-art methods for points, curves, and inside corners are on pages 13 to 22. Patterns begin on a 9" square, cut down after completion to finished size.

Might a novice begin on *Fancy Appliqué*'s Lesson One? Sure! This would be like apprenticing oneself to a pastry chef rather than to a grill cook—and there can be no harm in skipping the meat and potatoes of *Appliqué 12 Easy Ways!* when the author's favorite methods and your full enjoyment are well-served here. (Even if studied later, the broad spectrum of basics presented in *Appliqué 12 Easy Ways!* will enhance your skills.) For those already well-versed in appliqué, this book's *haute cuisine* challenges are irresistible. Each exercise encourages a playful exploration, beginning with that favorite appliqué motif, the heart. In this relaxed mode, you (like Einstein, whose Theory of Relativity "came to him" while shaving) will discover astonishing beauty!

Fancy Appliqué makes a fine teaching text. The Appendix facilitates this with course formats. Your own first goal, however, may be to make a Fancy Appliqué Sampler or Album Quilt. Virtually every quilt option for setting squares—from plain sets to fancy—invites consideration for displaying this collection on a theme. Whether a wall quilt, a Victorian Crazy-style throw, or a bed quilt as full of blocks as Jane Stickle's Civil War quilt, your Fancy Sampler Quilt will voice your thoughts through yet another century's turn. Lisa McCulley designed original sets for this book's dramatic Fancy Sampler Quilt I (photo, page 4) and Fancy Sampler Quilt II (photo, page 11). She machine quilted them with custom motifs. Those quilts' specifications and sets accompany the appliqué blocks in the Pattern Section. Might the twenty-first century's best attended quilt shows boast a new category, the Fancy Sampler Quilt? If so, I hope to admire your fancywork there!

———

Completing a quilt casts honor upon its maker. For a quiltmaker, a finished quilt is the best reward. Earning an honorary degree through the lessons of *Fancy Appliqué* may appeal, though, as a private measure of accomplishment. Multiple recreational activities today sponsor masters programs. You probably know a "master swimmer" or a "master gardener." As quiltmakers, might we also bestow a Master of Arts in Appliqué? And what can be the harm, if done for the pleasure of a high goal set and then well met? *Fancy Appliqué* intends honorable challenge. Lessons 1 through 9 can qualify as your *baccalaureate*. When completed, why not give yourself a Bachelor of Arts? It seems worthwhile to acknowledge (either in class or to oneself) a liberal arts education in appliqué, faithfully accomplished!

Lesson 10 tests your skills on a miniature rose approached four different ways, then names success a Master of Arts in Appliqué. And if some appliqué rarity intrigues you passionately, why not formulate its pursuit as a philosophical query? Such research (Lessons 11 and 12) can fashion a thesis proposal. Then, if substantive learning occurs, go ahead (and just for you) grant yourself a Ph.D. in Appliqué. At a university graduation, this award would be called a "Doctor of Philosophy, *honoris causa*"—for honorary causes. That title surely seems to fit our task!

What's a "fancy"?

fancy, *n.; pl.* **fancies,** from the Latin *phantasia,* an idea, notion. Fancy can be either a whim or a more involved concept, a fancy. The term has a happy connotation. We can take a fancy to something. We can become fanciful and give our imagination free play. Play is at the heart of fancywork and while it comes naturally to children, we adults sometimes need to coax it. My own offspring are past childhood now, but last summer a little girl approached the beach chair where I sat writing and, standing with clear eyes leveled at mine, engaged me in conversation, initially by thrusting at me a wee wedge of shell. Caught by surprise, I innocently entered into her fancy:

What have you got there? I asked. *Is it a broken shell?*
No, it is a piece of pie.
Really?
Yes, it is the last piece of pie.
Who made it?
The sea fairy. She baked it early, early this morning. It smelled so good that bird friends begged pieces. This is the last one.
My goodness!
Would you like it?
The last one? (Her daddy called, "Come on, Emily, come with us now.")
You can have it.
Eyes toward her dad, she poked her arm out backhand to me, the shell piece served up on her flattened palm. I took it.
Why thank you!
I said, and smiled at that sea fairy named Emily, skip-dancing off to catch up with her parents. I looked at the sand below my chair. Just for a moment, my eyes searched for a second piece of pie.

—

"Every child is an artist," said Picasso. "The problem is how to remain an artist once he grows up." So part of doing fancywork must be to trust in our imaginings, to settle in a safe and comfortable well-lit spot, to take a relaxing breath, and to play just with the cloth and color, the needle and thread. Surely in working on *Fancy Appliqué*'s squares, your play instincts will frolic in fancy!

Fancy Sampler Quilt II
Blocks by Elly Sienkiewicz; quilt designed, pieced, and quilted by
Lisa D. McCulley, 65½" x 65½", 1998

Part I

Setting Stitchery's Stage

"Well begun is half done."

— Great-aunt Orpha Hall Hamilton

Materials and supplies needed for each pattern are listed by lesson. Help with hard-to-find materials is in Sources on page 140.

Appliqué Supplies

- **Needles and Pins**: Milliners needles #10 and #11 are suggested for appliqué. (Straw and milliners are different names for the same needle.) Use 1½" straight pins or small safety pins to pin the appliqué layer to foundation cloth from the back. Use ¾" straight pins for pin-basting appliqués from the right side.
- **Thread**: Fine (50-60 weight) cotton or silk thread is ideal for fine appliqué. "Invisible" (100 weight) silk in warm or cool neutrals used with Appliqué Academy #11 straw needles (see Sources, page 140) is a magical combination for ultra-fine stitches.
- **Scissors**: Small (5") cut-to-the-point scissors.
- **Markers**: Fine mechanical pencil or brown Pigma™ Micron 01 pen for marking the background square.
- **Templates**: Heat-bondable freezer paper is always suitable for appliqué templates and window templates. (A window template is the paper frame that remains after the appliqué template shape is cut out. Use a window template to select that portion of a printed fabric best suited for an appliqué.) For greater ease, use uncut 8½" x 11" Avery® labels (photocopiable) or contact paper. Both are self-sticking papers. (For ease and economy, *Fancy Appliqué*'s block instructions call for contact paper template construction.)
- **Finishing Templates**: Transparent plastic template: 9" square for cutting background prior to appliqué; square cut to your quilt's finished block size for marking the seamline.

Embellishment Supplies

Embroidery or Crewel Needles (same needle by different names): While actual size differs with the manufacturers, the following are approximate needle sizes for carrying the embellishment threads, flosses, and silk ribbons used in *Fancy Appliqué*:

- Use a size 1 embroidery needle (or a #22 chenille needle) for size 3 (thick) pearl cotton embroidery thread.
- Use a size 3 embroidery needle (or a #24 chenille) for size 5 (medium) pearl cotton embroidery thread.
- Use a size 4 embroidery needle (or a #26 chenille) for size 8 (fine) pearl cotton or for DMC® Antique Gold or Antique Silver embroidery thread (the variety that comes on a spool).
- Chenille needles: use #22 or #24 for 4mm silk embroidery ribbon. Use #20 or #22 for 7mm silk embroidery ribbon.
- Use a size 7 or 8 embroidery needle (or a #26 chenille needle) with machine weight metallic thread.
- Use a #11 sharps or milliners needle for beading. Mill Hill® seed beads have been used throughout this book.
- Use an all-purpose 6" embroidery hoop, or use a larger 10" hoop for silk ribbon or bead embroidery, basting extenders onto this book's 9" foundation square so that the embroidery is not crushed.

Mixed Media Appliqué Supplies

Heat-setting is suggested for all pigments; however, washing is not advised for mixed media appliqué.

- Pigma Micron pens are acid-free, permanent, and non-transient. They are ideal for writing and drawing on cloth.

- Pigma™ Brush pens paint on permanent color with a fine brush tip.
- Prismacolor® Pencils are ideal for dry shading of cloth.
- Aquarelles® are superior colored pencils for color drawing or for shading and can be painted over with water for a watercolor effect.
- Sakura of America's Cray-Pas® have a wide color range for stencil-shading. Heat set, they are permanent under cold water. Delta's Oil Paintstiks® are permanent after heat-setting. Oil stencil-shading as an appliqué art is taught in *Papercuts and Plenty*.

Block Preparation and Completion

Thirty-nine patterns are given in the Pattern Section (pages 110 to 130) for the forty-four blocks. There, block preparation and pattern transfer are taught. While *Appliqué 12 Easy Ways!* provides a multitude of methods for appliquéing a single pattern, *Fancy Appliqué* advocates one appliqué technique for each different pattern. The initial step remains consistent: On a light box, trace the appliqué shape onto contact paper, cut the shape, and finger-press it to the appliqué fabric (Layer A), right-side up. Next, pin Layer A to the background square (Layer B, also right-side up). Use two or more pins to avoid pivoting. Alternatively, big-stitch baste the two layers together.

BLOCK COMPLETION

1.**Pressing**: Lay the fully stitched block face down on a worn terry towel. Wet a thin cotton press cloth with MagicSizing® or other spray starch. Iron the block until the press cloth is dry. (Avoid pressing too hard, for this may draw attention to the seam beneath the appliqué.)

2.**Cutting block to size**: Lay a transparent square (the size of your quilt block's finished seamline) on the back of your block, centering it by eye over the appliqué's underside. Draw the block's seamline around the template, then trim the excess to a ¼" seam allowance.

Appliqué's Three Stitch Sisters

Forever at your service are the non-decorative "tack" and "blind" appliqué stitches. The first, the tack stitch, is our gal Friday. Anything that can be appliquéd, she can do. The second, the blind stitch, is more specialized: bring her in for speed or invisibility (the "blindness" in the blind stitch). Rely on the can-do tack stitch, though, for inside corners and outside points. Both the tack and the blind stitch are matriarchs with many descendants, each introduced in *Appliqué 12 Easy Ways!* Come, meet my favorite three appliqué stitches here—stitch sisters for all your appliqué seasons!

SISTER TACK STITCH CATCHING-THE-EDGE

We'll call her tack stitch for short. She looks and functions like a staple. As a staple, she clamps down the edge of the appliqué and secures it to the foundation.

1. **Start the Stitch**: Start with an 18" to 24" thread, knotted. Begin the stitch (a) from underneath the foundation. Pierce the needle up through the foundation (b), the appliqué seam (c), and through the appliqué itself (d), leaving a tiny fold beyond it.

2. **Completing the Stitch**: The start of the stitch is like the left leg of a staple. To complete the staple/stitch, pull the thread straight over to the appliqué edge and slip the needle's point under the fold (e) and down as though into the hole where it first came up.

3. **And On to a New Stitch**: Scrape your finger beneath the block and move the needle forward ¹⁄₁₆", then repeat Step 1. Right-handers stitch from right to left, while left-handers stitch from left to right. Finish each stitch with a tug and keep all forward motion on the back of the block.

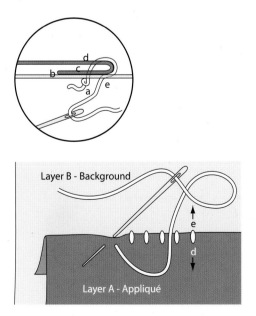

Fig.1 Sister Tack Stitch Catching-the-Edge

Note: Nix Thread Slither: If thread becomes worrisomely short but you have no time to rethread, you can tie a loop knot at the eye (f). This also keeps silk thread from falling out of the needle.

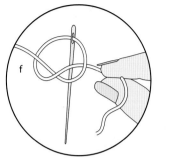

Fig. 2 Securing the thread into the eye of the needle

SISTER INVISIBLE RUNNING STITCH

Visualize the blind stitch family's quickest, easiest member as an invisible running stitch taken just under the seamline, threaded beneath the fold, joining the seam allowance and the foundation fabric with a steady nip and pull (g). Three in and out "nips" to one firm "pull" saves time. Complete the pull by taking a tiny tack stitch (h). Pierce up through Layer A, pull the thread, and reinsert the needle under the seam's fold. Resume the invisible running stitch.

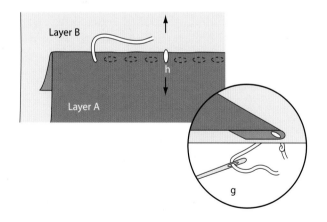

Fig. 3 Sister Invisible Running Stitch

SISTER VISIBLE RUNNING STITCH

Closely related although no longer a blind stitch, the (visible) running stitch is the quickest, easiest appliqué stitch of all! Take the running stitch just inside the appliqué's folded edge (i) and stitch through all three cloth layers. Make the top of the stitch tiny and leave twice its length between stitches.

For speed, load several stitches onto your needle before pulling it through. This stitch's textural rhythm defines an appliqué's edge.

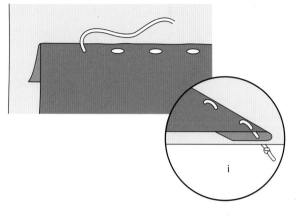

Fig. 4 Sister Visible Running Stitch

Adept Needleturn Appliqué

THE NEEDLETURN PROCESS

Needleturn means progressively tucking the seam under with the needle, inch by inch, as you are about to appliqué that inch down. The tack, blind, and visible running stitch all suit needleturn appliqué, although the tack stitch is always used for securing points and corners. Needleturn suits cutaway appliqué, reverse cutaway appliqué, and separate unit appliqué.

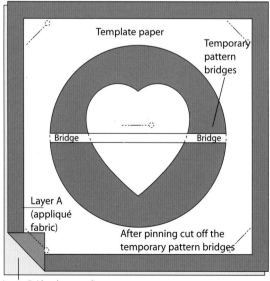

Fig. 5 Preparation A Pattern 1, "The Centered Heart," prepared for cutaway appliqué

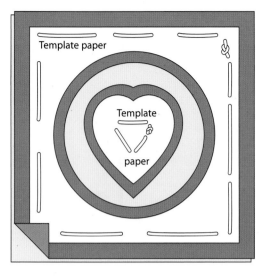

Fig. 6 Preparation B Pattern 1, "The Centered Heart," prepared for separate unit needleturn appliqué

CUTAWAY APPLIQUÉ

Cutaway appliqué begins with a pattern-marked cloth. The seam allowance is cut as you go, inches at a time; hence the name "cutaway" appliqué. Figure 7 shows a preparation for cutaway (sometimes called onlaid cutaway) appliqué: The paper template is adhered to Layer A's right side. Layer A is then placed (right-side up) over Layer B, the background cloth (also right-side up). The layers are pinned or big-stitch basted together. Cutaway appliqué has two principles:

Principle 1. Never cut around a point, always cut beyond a point—a generous inch past the point where possible. The cut must always continue in the same direction as the seam (a).

Principle 2. Never change the direction of your cut until the first side of a point is sewn (b). The uncut cloth itself will have stabilized the appliqué shape.

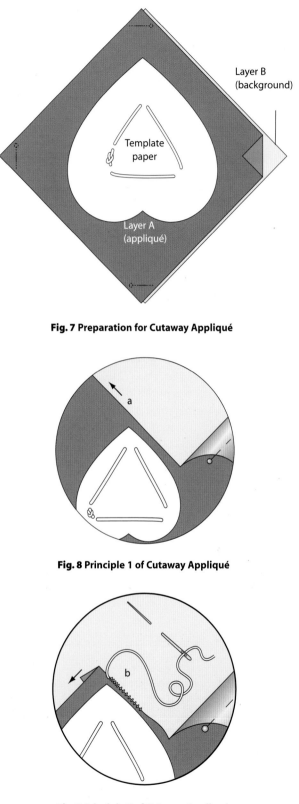

Fig. 7 Preparation for Cutaway Appliqué

Fig. 8 Principle 1 of Cutaway Appliqué

Fig. 9 Principle 2 of Cutaway Appliqué

REVERSE CUTAWAY APPLIQUÉ

Figure 10 illustrates reverse cutaway appliqué's preparation, as Figure 13 illustrates its finishing. Shuffle ("reverse") the order, first putting Layer A (right-side up) on the table, then covering it with Layer B (right-side up). This reversed order changes where the seams lie and makes reverse the easiest way to appliqué predominantly curved shapes as in Pattern 4, "The Hurry-up Heart." In between block preparation and finishing, the needleturn appliqué (pages 14 to 22) of points, curves, and corners is always the same.

1. As a right-hander, cut the heart's left seam allowance (see Figure 11) first, appliquéing the left before cutting the right.

2. Adjust the width of the seam allowance: cut it a touch narrower (³⁄₁₆") on the curves, wider (a full ¼") at the inside (b) and outside (a) points. Why? Because a curve turns best with a smaller seam and a point turns best with a larger seam. The ³⁄₁₆"-wide seam on the curve (Figure 11) includes the seamline fold, leaving a scant ⅛" seam allowance to tuck under.

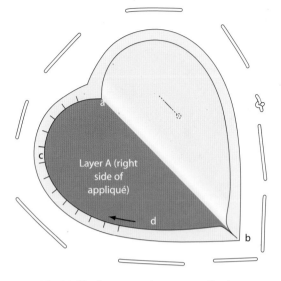

Fig. 11 Clipping a curved reverse appliqué seam

3. Clip two-thirds into the curved seam's depth (c). Clip every ¼" (or at the curve's deepest parts).

4. Clip three-quarters into the inside point's seam (b), bisecting it and giving equal cloth to the right and left seam allowances. *Never cut a needleturned corner right to the paper template!*

5. Begin reverse needleturn appliqué on the heart's straight at (d). Appliqué from right to left. As you progress you'll naturally change how you hold the block (Figure 12). Note that where the seam has been cut, needleturned, and appliquéd, a tiny piping-like fold now outlines the paper template (e).

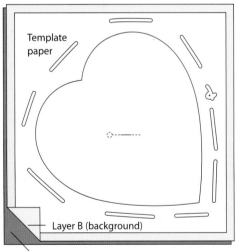

Fig. 10 Preparation for Pattern 4, "The Hurry-up Heart"

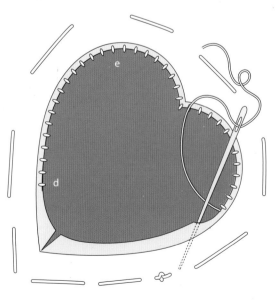

Fig. 12 As you needleturn from right to left, the position of the block changes. The seam remains a tiny fold sticking out beyond the paper template, never under it.

6. When the appliqué is completed, remove the basting and template. Turn the block over (Figure 13). Cut Layer A's seam to ⅛" (narrower than Layer B's seamline), so that B masks A from the front. This prevents A from showing, shadow-like, around B in the finished quilt. Note that the Layer B clipped seam has opened to lie smooth and flat (f). This lack of bulk on the curve is the genius of reverse appliqué.

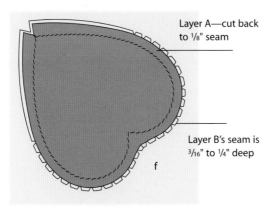

Layer A—cut back to ⅛" seam

Layer B's seam is 3/16" to ¼" deep

f

Fig. 13 From the wrong side you can see how flat the seams lie in reverse appliqué. There is no bulk on the curves.

NEEDLETURN IN MOTION

Like a country road clean-slicing through corn fields, starting needleturn on a straight line in the pattern means easy stitching. The longer the straight-line start, the better for warming up your appliqué. In Figure 14, the needleturned seamline follows an imaginary line, just beyond the paper template. Always appliqué several threads beyond the paper template, where you can see and control the seamline, not blind, underneath the paper's edge. As your work progresses, the appliqué seamfold will outline the paper shape's edge.

Angular Inside Corners

1. A right-hander will needleturn the seam from right to left, beginning above a corner (a) and stopping ½" short of each corner (b) before turning it under.
2. Cut three-quarters into the corner seam allowance, dividing it equally. (Stop at the imaginary turn line—Figure 14's dashed line.)
3. Rest the needle's shank over the right seam flap (c). The needle's tip moves freely under the appliqué, but over the foundation fabric. Its upper shank lies across the right-hand seam allowance, catching it, ready to swoop it under.

4. Completely cover the needle (c) with your thumb. Pinch hard. Then, still pinching, sweep the seam (d) under.

Needleturning an Inside Corner

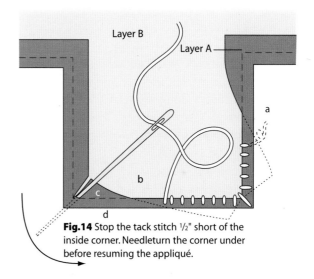

Layer B

Layer A

a

b

c

d

Fig.14 Stop the tack stitch ½" short of the inside corner. Needleturn the corner under before resuming the appliqué.

5. Lighten your pinch to withdraw the needle; then resume the pressure. Tack stitch up to your thumb. Nothing different happens until the last stitch (stitch 3-4 in Figure 15) before the inside corner.
6. While you're pinching, note Figure 15's X-ray view of the tucked seam. In Step 9, a unique second stitch will lasso the corner seam's raw edge, rolling it under crisply!

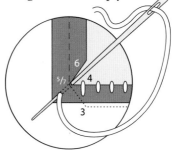

Fig. 15 The needle always pierces down into Layer B to complete a tack stitch —except when completing the first stitch of an outside corner. The needle pierces up through Layer B and then Layer A to begin the next tack stitch at 5. This stitch is taken twice. The second time (at #7) the needle slips under Layer A (only) and pierces up again through Layer A (only) at #7.

7. Begin 3-4, the last stitch before the corner, 1½ needle shanks deeper (closer to the template) into the appliqué. Come up at 3 and re-enter the background directly opposite at 4.

8. At the bottom of the corner's slit, come up at 5 (three needle shanks deep toward the template).

9. Finish the stitch directly opposite, slipping the needle under Layer A's edge at 6 (⁶⁄₈). But this time *don't* re-enter the background: Slip the needle under Layer A only and bring it up, just through Layer A again, at 7 (⁵⁄₇). Pull this stitch tightly, halving its length. Shortening this stitch rolls the corner's raw edge under.

10. Needleturn the corner's left seam under. Begin the final slightly long stitch there by entering the background (Layer B) two threads under the rolled fold at 8 (⁶⁄₈) and coming up through Layer B and Layer A at 9.

11. Complete this stitch at 10. Congratulations! You've tidily traversed that corner valley and are needle-hiking on your way once again.

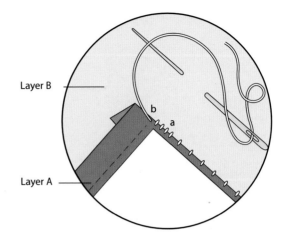

Fig.17 Needleturning a Point

Layer B

Layer A

Preparing to turn the point

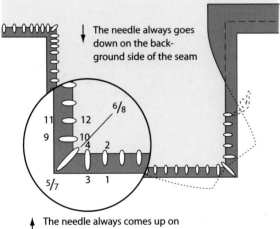

↓ The needle always goes down on the background side of the seam

11 12   ⁶⁄₈
9   10   2
     4
   3   1
⁵⁄₇

↑ The needle always comes up on the template side of the seam.

Fig.16 At #8 pierce the needle down through Layer B and up at #9 through Layer B and Layer A.

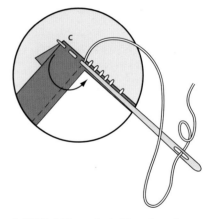

Step 1. PUSH: A. Woven Push: (Thread needle into the seam allowances to control the push.)

PERFECT NEEDLETURNED POINTS

Oh, the joy of a successful point! It can be forever yours by the six-step formula of "Push + Pivot + Pinch + Pull + Point to Point + Stitch in Place = A Perfect Point!"

To prepare for Figure 17's formula point:

• Take close stitches the last ¼" before a point (a).

• Take the final stitch one stitch beyond the paper template's point (b).

• Pull the background cloth firmly over your left forefinger, securing it with your middle finger so it doesn't budge. This means that when you "push" the appliqué seams down and around, the seams will pivot, but the background will not move.

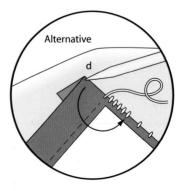

Alternative

B. Alternative Push: (Use a round wooden toothpick or fine embroidery scissors to push the seams under. Layer B is held taut by forefinger.)

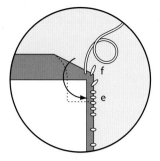

Step 2. PIVOT: Pushing, pivot both seam allowances down and around until stopped by the sewn seam (e). Do this with such assurance that the last stitches are loosened (f).

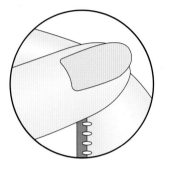

Step 3 PINCH: Pinch to crease the fold made by Steps 1 and 2.

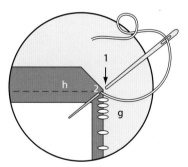

Step 4. PULL: Pull the thread at the corner to tug the point and tighten its stitches.

Step 5. POINT TO THE POINT: Reinsert the needle two threads beyond the point (1) and come up at 2. Next tuck seam (h) under so it descends in a straight line from the point.

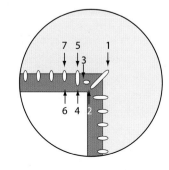

Step 6. STITCH IN PLACE

Formula for a Perfect Point

Step 1: PUSH

The push takes control of the exposed seam allowances, the ones you want tucked smoothly beneath the point. Always push close to the raw edge and close to the fold—never mid-seam allowance.

A. The Woven Push: Weave ("push") the needle in and out of the two exposed seams (c). Then pivot the seams under with this "in control" needle!

B. The Alternative Push: Push using a round toothpick or embroidery scissors. With the sharp tip, push down hard (close to the fold, close to the raw edge) against the seam so these seams pivot under as one. (This is my favorite method.)

Step 2: PIVOT

Push down and around, jamming the seamfold to a stop (e) against the fine stitches. The motion of the pivot is that of making a "hospital corner" with a bedsheet.

Step 3: PINCH

Cover the turned point completely with your thumb. And because you previously pushed so assertively down and to the right, now push, thumb pinched to forefinger, up to the left.

Step 4: PULL

Remove your thumb. If you did everything right, your point will look terribly wrong. The last stitches taken (f) will have been pulled loose. Now pull the hanging thread (g). Pulled by that thread, the fold should magically slip out into a finely turned point.

Step 5: POINT TO THE POINT

Pierce Layer B two threads beyond the point (1), bringing the needle up through Layer A at 2. Before continuing to Step 6, tuck seam (h) under so that the descent from the peak mirrors the ascent. Tuck with a toothpick or embroidery scissors if the needle is inadequate to the task.

Step 6: STITCH IN PLACE

Stab-stitch (up at 2, down one thread to the left at 3) to flatten. Bring the needle up two threads further left at 4, then resume the tack stitch's familiar nip and pull.

Practice ensures success: push, pivot, pinch, pull, point to point, and stitch in place for a PERFECT POINT!

Miniaturization

Miniaturization—the known presented on a Lilliputian scale—is by nature fancy. What would I keep the same for miniature appliqué? I would do needleturn appliqué marked by paper on the top and use the tack stitch. In most cases, I would use separate unit appliqué, but might trim the seam allowance as I go, which is to say, I would start larger to finish smaller. Yes, I would take my finest stitches with my finest #11 milliners needle and 100 weight silk thread. While I was at it, I would start with a fine cotton cloth with a high thread count and my finest embroidery scissors. And unless there was reason not to, I would mark my background with a Pigma Micron 005 pen, giving myself a fine clear line to guide my needleturn on both appliqué and foundation cloths. Here are a few more mini-basics:

1. You must leave a ³⁄₁₆" seam allowance at both inside and outside points. Sometimes you can clip a wedge from an outside point turned from the right before sewing it on the left.

2. Try taking two tiny stitches (instead of one) past the paper template's corner for a super-sharp point.

3. You can get away with a scant ⅛" seam, even as little as a ¹⁄₁₆" seam, if the thread count is high and the grain placement favors it—or if you paint the cloth with a sealant, like clear nail polish, before cutting the seam down. (What about "pattern impossible" whose so-sharp point cannot be sewn? Know that this is the pattern-maker's problem, not yours!)

4. On a tiny tight curve, like a ½" circle, only a small (⅛") seam will needleturn under smoothly. Alternatively, turn such a circle by gathering a ¼" seam around a file card template, spray starch the edge, iron from the back, clip the thread, and remove the paper. Since ¼" is half the circle's diameter, the piece will be self-stuffed by the seam allowances.

Needleturning Curves

Preparation tips for needleturned curves are illustrated by Figure 18.

a. Cut a narrower (between ³⁄₁₆" and ⅛") seam allowance on an outside curve.

b. Cut a ¼" to ³⁄₁₆" seam allowance on an inside curve.

c. Clip two-thirds deep and perpendicular to a concave curved seam, clipping the deepest parts of the curve.

d. Start needleturn on the descent of a convex curve or on the ascent of a concave curve.

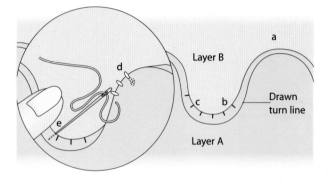

Fig. 18 Needleturning Curves

FOR A RIGHT-HANDER TO NEEDLETURN A CURVE

1. With the needle's point, catch the seam (e) and pull it under toward you from left to right with regal authority (it helps). On an outside curve, pull the seam under with the needle's point and pinch in the fold to hold it: pull and pinch, pull and pinch. On an inside curve, use the shank of the needle to smooth the seam under.

2. Move your left thumb to the right to hold this self-assured turn (it will become so).

3. Tack stitch up to within an ⅛" before your thumb; stop and lift your thumb. Needleturn the next half inch, hold it, and stitch again. Always stop ⅛" before your thumb; stitching all of a turn at one time encourages peaks. Lift your thumb and use your needle like a windshield wiper, reaching beyond the already turned ⅛", catching the seam underneath and changing its direction, so that the turning seam follows the changing curve—one stitch at a time!

4. If your curve inadvertently peaks, return to the culprit and, using that same windshield wiper motion, snag the underneath seam on needle's point, pull it smooth, then finger-press it to flat perfection!

Classic Curved Corners

The angular corner we mastered earlier (Figures 14-16) deserves a bit of "How green was my valley" nostalgia, for rarely are corners as straight-on and accessible as is the right angle corner. A U-turn corner is the classic "tight corner." But we'll master it, too! It must, of course, be clipped, for it is an inside curve *in extremis*. Figure 19 shows a U-turn's seam allowance clipped like a 1960's peace sign. The clip's forks cut the curved seam two-thirds deep, allowing the seam to flare back under the turn line, yet still offering a solid edge for rolling under. Sweep the seam under (Figure 20) catching the clip with the needle's shank. In this case, start high on the left side, pulling the seam under and finger-pressing it down. You may have to repeat this to train the cloth.

Figure 21 shows the U-turn's seamline appliquéd by a strung-bead series of tack stitches. Each slightly long stitch begins two threads under the seamfold, then emerges from the appliqué three threads beyond. A tug on the emerging thread curls the seam even as the next stitch is begun. These taut rolling stitches hem the curved corner like turning the edge on a silk scarf.

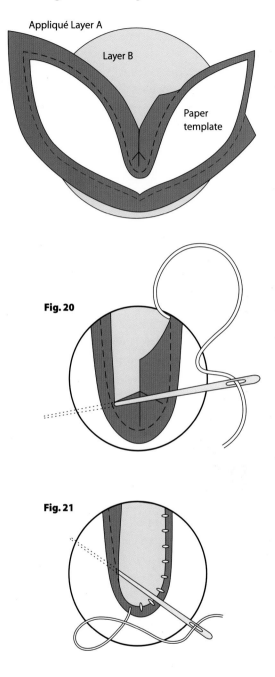

Fig.19 Needleturning a U-turn Corner

Appliqué Layer A

Layer B

Paper template

Fig. 20

Fig. 21

CURVED CORNER MEETS STRAIGHT STEM

This combination, illustrated in Figure 22, is a match made in heaven, for it simplifies the construction of classic patterns throughout the *Baltimore Beauties* ® series. I love this cutaway appliqué concept whereby leaves and stems can be sewn in one layer, from one piece of cloth, rather than layered from separate units. A decade after *Baltimore Beauties and Beyond, Studies in Classic Album Quilt Appliqué, Volume I,* was first published, few remember that the preponderance of cutaway patterns today is more a result of that series' redrafted interpretations than of the classic appliqués themselves. "Curved corner meets straight stem" is a simple pair: One partner is half of an "angular inside corner" (pages 17-18), the other is half of a curved corner. They never work better together than when growing a leaf out of a stem, illustrated in Figure 22.

1. Since right-handers always approach an outside point (or an inside corner) from the right side, the stitcher would first have passed through the right angle corner (a) beneath the leaf. As she rounds the leaf's tip (having left it breathtakingly sharp) her scissors pause before cutting the inside corner at the leaf's upper side.

   Note: The principle of a connected leaf/stem is: "When extra seam allowance is needed, it must always come out of the leaf, not out of the stem." If the stem's seam allowance is not given a 45° angle flap, the stem cannot emerge on the same straight line above the leaf as it does below it. Taking extra seam allowance out of the stem itself would leave it scoopy, not straight. On the other hand, taking extra seam allowance out of the leaf just makes the leaf/stem connection breathtakingly fine. Therefore, cut the upper leaf/stem juncture with a diagonal cut to the corner as shown at (b).

2. By needleturn, sweep the curved seam under from the corner to the right, finger-pressing it beneath your thumb at (c). Take the same series of slightly long tack stitches, pulled tightly, as just described for the classic curved corner, page 21.

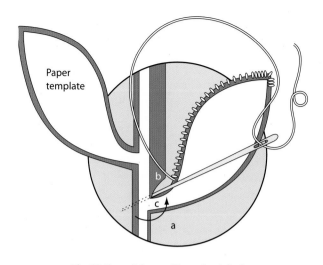

Fig. 22 Curved Corner Meets Straight Stem

3. The corner at its stem juncture is stitched by the same long stitch taken twice (23, d) that we encountered at the angular inside corner taught earlier. With one final slightly long stitch (e) taken to the left, the curved corner has met the stem. This happy couple can now be seen on virtually every turn of the twenty-first century Baltimore-style Album appliqué quilt. The stage thus set, let's discover the joys of our own millennial Fancy Sampler Album. And—for the joy of it—let's award ourselves with some higher learning degrees as we progress!

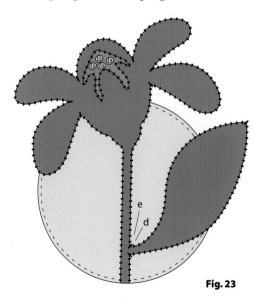

Fig. 23

Imagination is as important as knowledge.

—Albert E. Einstein

Part II: The Lessons

LESSON 1

Dancing the Heart Two-Step

O give me new figures! I can't go on dancing
The same that were taught me ten seasons ago…
Invent something new, and you'll set me a skipping:
I want a new figure to dance with my Dear!

-T.H. Bayly, *Quadrille à la Mode*

The Two-Step is a simple design repeat: a step down by reverse appliqué, then a step up by onlaid appliqué. Like a showy performer, improvise with your own signature style—Fraktur, Cloisonné, or Twist/Entwine—and fancify needlework's dance from her very first step!

Materials

For basic supplies, see Appliqué Supplies, page 12.

PATTERN 1
Appliqué (Layer A): 9" square of large-scale cotton print
Background (Layer B): 9" square of small-scale cotton print

PATTERN 2
(Pattern 2, "The Bountiful Heart" uses the Pattern 1 template)
Appliqué (Layer A): 9" square of large-scale cotton print. Use a window template (page 12) to center printed bounty (like the grapes pictured) within the heart appliqué.
Background (Layer B): Two 4 ¾" x 9" rectangles of cotton cloth, machine sewn into a 9" background square. (Press both seams toward the bottom of the block.)

PATTERN 3
Appliqué (Layer A): A scrap (7" square or so) of variegated cotton
Background (Layer B): 9" square of cotton solid

Supplies for Embellishment

PATTERNS 1 AND 2
Antique gold embroidery thread

PATTERNS 2 AND 3
Variegated 4mm and 7mm silk embroidery ribbon; seed beads.

PATTERN 2
Size 8 pearl cotton thread

Fancywork Design Approaches

Fancywork is like *haute cuisine*—its ingredients are basic to standard fare, but unique combinations and embellishments lift it above the ordinary. Three design approaches follow; each guarantees irrepressibly fresh fancywork!

Fraktur

Silhouetted shapes, watercolored, characterize Pennsylvania German frakturs. While the word fraktur relates to broken type used in early printing presses, in fancywork appliqué it formulates a fractured shape, ideally a simple one like the heart, that most beloved of appliqué motifs.

Cloisonné

n.—*A colored decoration made of enamels poured into the divided areas in a design, outlined with wire or metal strips.*

Cloisonné, as a fancywork appliqué concept, invites edge-defining embroidery. Any outlining stitches beloved of crazy-quilters would do. Metallic thread and this lesson's crewel stitch embellish many *Fancywork Appliqué* blocks.

Twist/Entwine

Twisting a clipped seam allowance to reduce bulk and flatten the seam is a couturier's technique. With sinuous style, Nancy Pearson has popularized what we'll call "twist/entwine" as a tool of appliqué. This technique is most useful when it enhances a leaf curve or twining ribbons. You'll perform it perfectly, led step by step in Pattern 3!

Fig. 24 Composition Contemplation: Which of these fraktur hearts might include reverse appliqué? Which heart might be reverse appliquéd to a pre-pieced foundation cloth? Which would best be enhanced by cloissoné-like embroidery, outline-stitched around the edge?

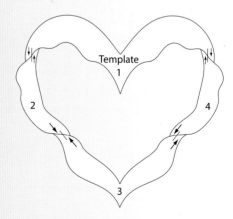

Fig. 25 Pattern 3 ("Ellen's Valentine") showing the templates traced onto contact paper. Note that prior to cutting the templates apart, the numbers, seam slash lines, and directional arrows have been drawn on each template unit.

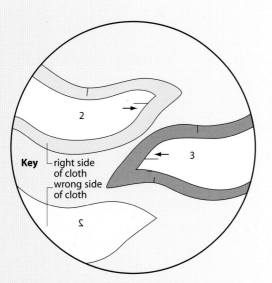

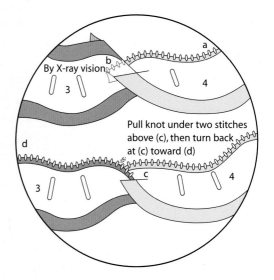

Fig. 26 Template pieces pressed to the appliqué cloth. Note the full ⅛" seam over curves and the full ³/₁₆" at points.

Fig. 28 Tip of the twist: Lift 3 back to continue stitching 4—from (a) to seam's end at (b). Secure, then clip your thread at (b). Re-knot and resume stitching just above (c). (This avoids a fray-causing knot at the seam-slash.) At (c), stitch toward (d). When you approach the bottom of the twist from the left, sew to seam's end at (e).

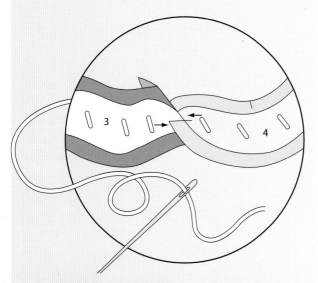

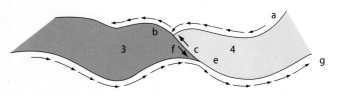

Fig. 29 Seam streams: Then start at (f) and stitch toward (g). The alphabetical order gives the stitching sequence while the arrows note the stitch flow's direction.

Fig. 27 Securing the appliqués: Pin, then baste through the template paper and foundation cloth. (Avoid the seam turn-under space.) Alternatively, draw around the template and remove the paper.

Sophisticated Stem (Crewel) Stitch

Caulfield's *Encyclopedia of Victorian Needlework* calls the "Crewel Stitch" what our contemporaries dub the Stem or Outline Stitch. While *Fancy Appliqué* uses crewel stitch as an umbrella term for simplicity, each has a useful difference. I disliked this stitch as a child, finding it difficult to control. The fact that it can sometimes arch unaccountably like an angry cat is resolved by where you hold the thread. When the thread is held below the needle, it is the stem stitch; when held above the needle, it is the outline stitch. The needle/thread sizes cited here are ideal for doing these stitches cloisonné-style around cotton appliqués.

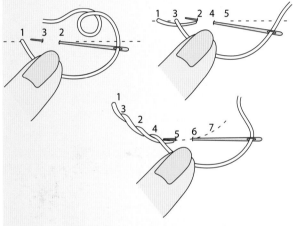

Fig. 30 The Crewel (*aka*) Stem Stitch

Stem Stitch

Use 18" of size 3 pearl cotton and a #4 Embroidery needle. Following Figure 30, knot the thread and start the stitch at 1. With your thumb, hold the thread consistently below the needle: "thread swung low" is what defines the stem stitch. Stitch from left to right, but keep the needle always pointing left as you stitch from 2 to 3. The stitch length from 2 to 3 should be small, about 1/16" to 1/8". Always put the needle into the cloth touching the bottom of the drawn line. Bring it out of the cloth touching the top of the drawn line. Continue. Enter at 4 and come up at 2. In this manner, a cable-like chain will result. Figure 30 shows the stem stitch worked on a concave curve. Some prefer to hold the piece vertically so the stem is worked upward (stitch away from yourself but with the needle pointing toward you). In that case the thread is always looped to the right of the needle. To thicken the stem, increase the needle's angle.

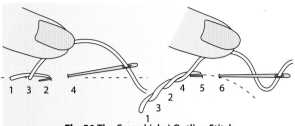

Fig. 31 The Crewel (aka) Outline Stitch

Outline Stitch

"Thread over head" defines the outline stitch. It is similar to the stem stitch, but the thread is consistently held above the needle as in Figure 31. By keeping the thread above (or when worked vertically, to the left of) the needle, the stitches will slope up to the right. The result may be a slightly straighter line. In Figure 31, the outline stitch is being worked on a convex curve. To outline an appliqué shape, first appliqué with fine thread by tack or running stitch, then go back and embroider the edge by outline stitch in a heavier thread.

What more? Edge-embroidery in decorative crewel stitch is a classic nineteenth century embellishment. On antique cotton appliqué quilts it is done as finely as with double sewing thread or a single strand of embroidery floss. Edge-stitching masks sewing mistakes and re-sculpts curves. When you thirst for more information on the surprising crewel stitch, find a detailed embroidery book and look up alternating stem stitch, whipped stem stitch, Portuguese knotted stem stitch, split stem stitch, encroaching stem stitch, and the outline stitch!

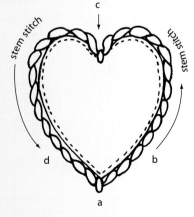

Fig. 32 Fine Points: Running stitch appliquéd, this heart is also stem stitch embroidered, cloisoné-style. Begun at (a) the stem stitch is worked upward and toward the right side. Conversely, one could begin at (a) and work upward and to the left, doing the outline stitch. Note that a fly stitch (page 120) lassos and anchors both the outward point (a), and the inward point (c).

"The Centered Heart" by Elly Sienkiewicz

Pattern 1 "The Centered Heart"

PROCEDURE

For full instructions, see Block Preparation and Pattern Transfer, page 110.

This block's fraktur is formal and simple: an encircled heart. Rich prints add a catchy rhythm to the heart/circle dance. Pattern 1 reinforces appliqué basics.

1. Cut a contact paper template of Pattern 1 (page 110).
2. Finger-press the template to Layer A, right-side up.
3. Center Layer B right-side down over Layer A (right-side down). From the wrong side, pin the layers together at the four corners and at the center (Figure 5).
4. Flip the stacked layers right-side up. Cut off the pattern bridges.
5. Baste the heart with three large stitches, then remove the center pin.

APPLIQUÉ APPROACH

For full instructions, see Adept Needleturn Appliqué, pages 14 to 22.

1. Sew the circle first. Use cutaway appliqué, cutting only 3" of seam allowance at a time, then clipping the seam two-thirds deep. Needleturn the edge under, appliquéing it by running stitch. For enviable results, review Visible Running Stitch, page 14.
2. Cutaway appliqué the heart by needleturn, using the versatile tack stitch (page 13). Figure 33 shows a right-hand start. Aim for a stunning display of a point, curves, and an inside corner!

FINISHING

See Block Completion, page 13. Refer to this hereafter for finishing all blocks.

I prefer to iron appliquéd blocks (even those silk ribbon embroidered), and not to trim away the background beneath the appliqué, leaving it intact for dimension. Trimming out behind onlaid appliqué flattens it, like patchwork.

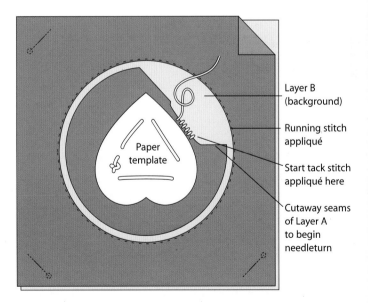

Fig. 33 Pattern 1 "The Centered Heart": When finished, the circle is ringed by beadlike stitches. Appliqué the heart next, again by cutaway, but for variation, tack stitch the needleturned edge. Right-handers always approach an inside or outside point from the right; the ideal right-hand start is shown.

"The Bountiful Heart" by Elly Sienkiewicz

Pattern 2 "The Bountiful Heart"

PROCEDURE

For full instructions, see Block Preparation and Pattern Transfer page, 110.

Use Pattern 1 again, but this time Get Fancy! Piece Layer B as specified in Materials, then pin-baste Layers A and B. Do the appliqué—all in running stitch for speed—then add stitchery cloisonné in metallic thread. Wreath the embroidered outline in silk ribbon leaves and berries to jazz up this two-step dance.

APPLIQUÉ APPROACH

For full instructions, see Adept Needleturn Appliqué, pages 14–22.

1. Running stitch appliqué the circle, then the heart, switching to the tack stitch only at the inside and outside corners.
2. Embellish the block cloisonné-style by embroidering all the seams. True, the very accomplished needlewoman can appliqué (i.e. stitch the turned-under seam to the background) using only embroidery thread and the crewel stitch, but we'll tackle appliqué by embroidery stitch in a later lesson.

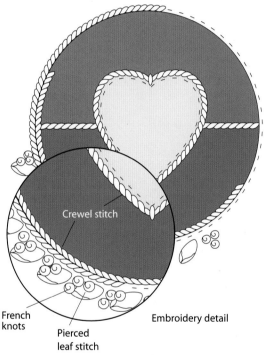

Fig. 34 Embellishing Pattern 2, "The Bountiful Heart"

EMBELLISHMENT

1. The crewel stitch (page 26) hugs the seam, nestling against it while worked in and out through the background. Antique gold embroidery thread outlines both heart and circle. A second row of crewel stitch (one strand of size 8 pearl cotton) frames the circle.
2. Silk ribbon embroidered leaves and berries wreath the circle's perimeter. The leaves are 7mm ribbon in pierced leaf stitch, the berries are 4mm ribbon French knots. The Embroidery Primer, pages 30-31, reviews those stitches.

"Ellen's Valentine" by Ellen Cieslak Sweeney

Pattern 3 "Ellen's Valentine"

PROCEDURE

For full instructions, see Block Preparation and Pattern Transfer, page 110.

Dimension, like miniaturization, has innate appeal. Though "Ellen's Valentine" never has more than two appliqué layers, its effect is voluptuous. Its lines and shading make as sensuous a shape of the heart as Georgia O'Keeffe makes of a lily. This is one of those perfect blocks where everything seems just right. Pattern 3's how-to is illustrated in this lesson's Twist/Entwine tutorial (pages 24-25).

EMBELLISHMENT

At heart's center, resting on French knotted 4mm silk embroidery ribbon, lies a bouquet. This lesson's Embroidery Primer (pages 30-31) teaches that flower arrangement's simple 4mm silk ribbon embroidered flowers (roses, rose buds, and wisteria).

And beautiful maidens moved down in the dance,
With the magic of motion and sunshine of glance.

—John Greenleaf Whittier

Embroidery Primer

Lazy daisy stitch

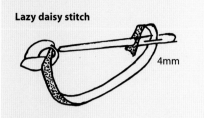

4mm

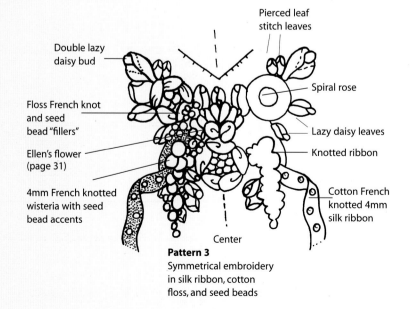

Lazy daisy bud
(stitch taken shorter and
more loosely)

4mm lazy daisy leaf
(stitch taken longer and
more tightly)

**Pierced leaf
stitch**

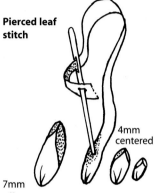

4mm
centered

7mm
off-center
pierced leaf stitch

Double lazy daisy

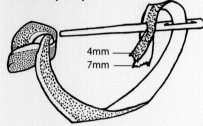

4mm
7mm

**Double lazy
daisy bud**

7mm pierced
leaf stitch
leaves

Double-threaded pierced leaf stitch

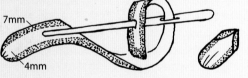

7mm

4mm

7mm

Maidenhair fern

**Off-center pierced
leaf stitch frond**

Embroidered folded leaf

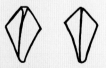

7mm silk embroidery ribbon
becomes folded when stitched up
(1) and down (2) at virtually the
same place

1 ↑
2 ↓

Double lazy
daisy bud

Floss French knot
and seed
bead "fillers"

Ellen's flower
(page 31)

4mm French knotted
wisteria with seed
bead accents

Pierced leaf
stitch leaves

Spiral rose

Lazy daisy leaves

Knotted ribbon

Cotton French
knotted 4mm
silk ribbon

Center

Pattern 3
Symmetrical embroidery
in silk ribbon, cotton
floss, and seed beads

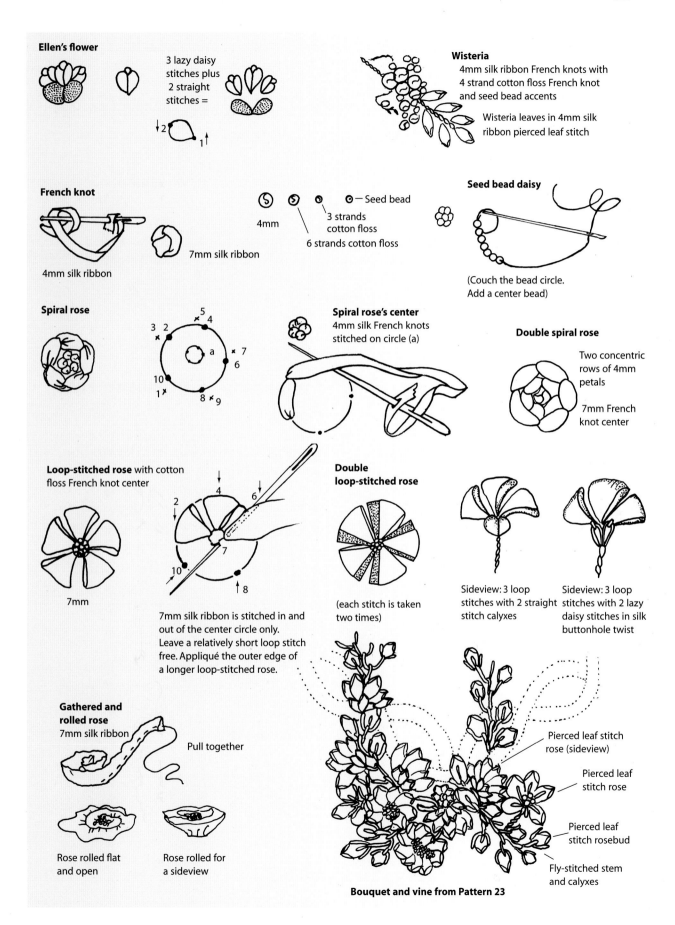

Ellen's flower

3 lazy daisy
stitches plus
2 straight
stitches =

↓2   1↑

Wisteria
4mm silk ribbon French knots with
4 strand cotton floss French knot
and seed bead accents

Wisteria leaves in 4mm silk
ribbon pierced leaf stitch

French knot

4mm silk ribbon

7mm silk ribbon

4mm

⊙ — Seed bead
3 strands
cotton floss
6 strands cotton floss

Seed bead daisy

(Couch the bead circle.
Add a center bead)

Spiral rose

5
3 2   4
a   7
6
10
1   8   9

Spiral rose's center
4mm silk French knots
stitched on circle (a)

Double spiral rose

Two concentric
rows of 4mm
petals

7mm French
knot center

Loop-stitched rose with cotton
floss French knot center

4
2   6
7
10   8

7mm

7mm silk ribbon is stitched in and
out of the center circle only.
Leave a relatively short loop stitch
free. Appliqué the outer edge of
a longer loop-stitched rose.

**Double
loop-stitched rose**

(each stitch is taken
two times)

Sideview: 3 loop
stitches with 2 straight
stitch calyxes

Sideview: 3 loop
stitches with 2 lazy
daisy stitches in silk
buttonhole twist

**Gathered and
rolled rose**
7mm silk ribbon

Pull together

Rose rolled flat
and open

Rose rolled for
a sideview

Pierced leaf stitch
rose (sideview)

Pierced leaf
stitch rose

Pierced leaf
stitch rosebud

Fly-stitched stem
and calyxes

Bouquet and vine from Pattern 23

LESSON 2

Hurry-Up Heart in Reverse

He is invariably in a hurry.
Being in a hurry is one of the tributes he pays to life.

— Elizabeth Babesco, *Balloons*

Curved motifs are simplest by reverse appliqué—and background ornament (collage or engraving) makes splendid even the simplest shape. Heart blocks appliquéd tonight promise embellishment tomorrow!

Materials

For basic supplies, see Appliqué Supplies, page 12.

PATTERN 4
Appliqué (Layer A): A scrap (9" square or so) of medium-scale cotton cloth
Background (Layer B): 9" square of large cotton print

PATTERN 5
Appliqué (Layer A): A scrap (9" square) of a cotton solid with a 2" x 6" organza ribbon basted diagonally across it
A second, more dramatic 2"-wide ribbon should be centered vertically on Layer A and basted over the organza ribbon
Background (Layer B): 9" square of medium-scale cotton print

PATTERN 6
Appliqué (Layer A): 9" square of a cotton solid
Background (Layer B): 9" square of a small to medium-scale cotton print

PATTERN 7
Appliqué (Layer A): 9" square of a large-scale cotton print
Background (Layer B): 9" square of cotton solid

PATTERN 8
Appliqué (Layer A): 9" square of pale cotton solid for photocopy engraving transfer
Background (Layer B): 9" square of cotton print

Supplies for Embellishment

PATTERN 6
Three 10" lengths of antique gold embroidery thread tied as one length into a tiny bow, its streamers separated by unwinding, then trimmed; green silk buttonhole twist for the stem; green 4mm silk embroidery ribbon for leaves; a rose colored 7mm silk embroidery ribbon for the rose.

PATTERN 7
Fancy threads: silk buttonhole twist, black Nymo®; rayon, cotton, and silk embroidery floss (separated into 1 or 2 strands); seed beads; 7mm x 18" of Mokuba® Pleated Satin Ribbon.

PATTERN 8
Carbon-based photocopy of Figure 38; seed beads; 4mm silk embroidery ribbon in two shades of green, variegated lavender, and variegated rose; black Pigma Micron 01 pen.

"The Hurry-up Heart" by Elly Sienkiewicz

Pattern 4 Heart

Pattern 4 "The Hurry-up Heart"

PROCEDURE

For full instructions, see Block Preparation and Pattern Transfer, page 110.

Reverse cutaway (a small seam tucked back into a large space) eases the heart's appliqué—and because it's easy, it's relatively quick. Reverse appliqué focuses on the base cloth's locket-like display. This block's print appliqué is cloissoné-edged by goldwork embroidery. In the overall quilt, this block's lack of contrast highlights more graphic adjacent blocks. To draw the eye to this block itself, use more contrasting fabrics for appliqué and background.

1. Trace Pattern 4 (page 111) onto a 6" square of contact paper.
2. Cut the shaded heart window template out and finger-press it, centered diagonally, onto Layer B.
3. Cut off the temporary pattern bridges.
4. Pin, then baste Layer B right-side up over Layer A, right-side up. See Figure 10 (page 16). The stationary window template will counteract a natural tendency to needleturn the seam back harder on one heart lobe than on the other.

Fig. 35 "The Hurry-up Heart" is edge embellished with crewel stitched (page 26) antique gold embroidery thread. Every half inch, trefoils of lazy daisy stitches (page 30) branch right and then left off this stem, and a cluster of cotton floss (3 strands) and silk buttonhole twist French knot fruits nestle in the crook of each branch.

APPLIQUÉ APPROACH

For step by step instructions, see Adept Needleturn Appliqué and Reverse Cutaway Appliqué, pages 14–22. Do Pattern 4's reverse appliqué by running stitch. Anchor the heart's inside and outside points by tack stitch.

EMBELLISHMENT

Stemming from the crewel stitch's cloissoné-like outline, goldwork trefoils and colored berry clusters repeat, wreath-like, around the heart. Figure 35's embroidery is shown at full scale. "The Hurry-up Heart" offers so simple a canvas for embellishment that it will tempt a quiltful!

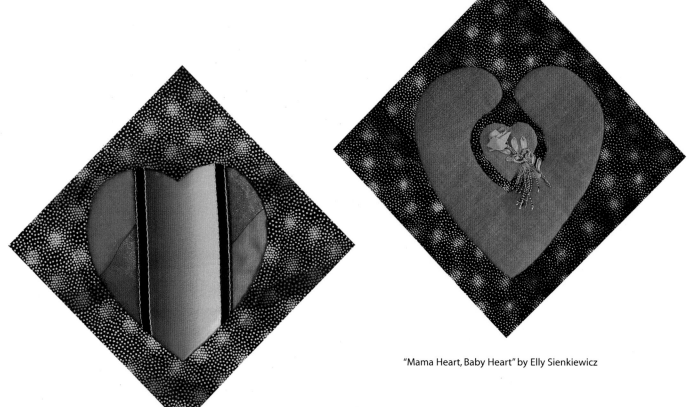

"Ribbon Collage Heart" by Elly Sienkiewicz

"Mama Heart, Baby Heart" by Elly Sienkiewicz

Pattern 5
"Ribbon Collage Heart"

PROCEDURE

Ribbon Collage Hearts are pure pleasure!

1. Baste the ribbon collage to Layer A as described in Pattern 5's materials list.
2. Make a contact paper window template using the heart from Pattern 4.
3. Follow Steps 1, 2, and 3 of Pattern 4.
4. Cut the heart seam allowance all around Layer B, removing the excess fabric at its center, creating a "window."
5. Use Step 4's window to locate Layer B over an appealing area of Layer A's ribbon collage. (Make sure there is sufficient Layer A seam under Layer B's appliqué.)
6. Pin, then baste Layer B over Layer A.
7. As with Pattern 4, use the running stitch and follow the pointers in Adept Needleturn Appliqué, pages 14 to 22.

Pattern 6
"Mama Heart, Baby Heart"

PROCEDURE

For full directions, see Block Preparation and Pattern Transfer, page 110.

High contrast diagonally set hearts are dramatic! Your quilt design will be the better for these at its center, in its corners, or placed in rows. Even this early on, consider the set options for your Fancywork Sampler Quilt.

APPLIQUÉ APPROACH

For full instructions, see Block Preparation and Pattern Transfer, page 110, and Adept Needleturn Appliqué, pages 14-22.

1. Cut a Pattern 6 (page 111) window template out of contact paper, transferring it to Layer A and removing the pattern bridges.
2. Pin, baste, and begin Mama Heart's reverse cutaway appliqué as in Figure 36 using the tack stitch.
3. Next, reverse cutaway appliqué Baby Heart. (Remove basting as needed.) Apply the basics of Miniaturization, taught on page 20.

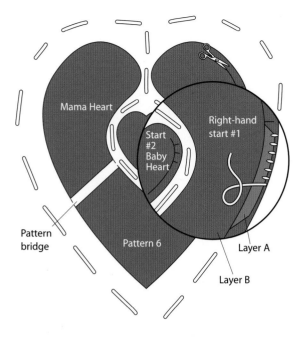

Fig. 36 Pattern 6 prepared for reverse cutaway appliqué

"Heart on the Edge" by Elly Sienkiewicz

EMBELLISHMENT

Elegantly simple, a long stem (stem stitched) holds a loop-stitched silk rose. Both the loop stitch and the pierced leaf stitch are taught on pages 30-31. Appliqué the loop-stitched rose and bow with silk thread to hold them in place.

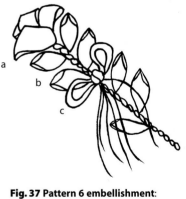

Fig. 37 Pattern 6 embellishment:
(**a**) 7mm ribbon loop-stitched rose
(**b**) 4mm ribbon pierced leaf stitched leaves
(**c**) Antique gold embroidery thread bow

Pattern 7 "Heart on the Edge"

PROCEDURE

Here a reverse-cutaway appliqué heart is running-stitch appliquéd to a showy large-scale print foundation, then the print is stitchery embellished to taste. A variety of threads and stitches can be used: the crewel stitch, chain stitch, and French knots. Also include a caught-thread stitch where the needle picks up every third thread from the cloth, in effect couching the embroidering thread. Pleat-satin ribbon (appliquéd with a seed bead on each stitch) is pictured, framing Pattern 7 (page 111). This formula (ribbon-trimmed heart, large-scale foundation print, and embellishment dictated by the print design) is simple yet stunning.

Heat-Transferred Engravings

1. Heat-bond a 9" square of freezer paper to the wrong side of Layer A. Fold the square into quarters, creasing it sharply to make registration marks.

2. Using a carbon-cartridged machine, photocopy Sadie Rose's engraving-like cameo, Figure 38.

3. Cut the cameo out of the photocopy (leaving a ½" outer margin of whitespace), then crease it into quarters, printed sides together, to make registration marks.

4. On a clean wooden board, center the cameo (printed side down) creases matching creases, on top of Layer A (right-side up). Pin together twice along one long margin of the copy to hold it steady during ironing.

5. With a hot (linen setting) dry iron, press the wrong side of the photocopy firmly. Push the point of the iron across the copy with circular motions, taking pains not to move the paper itself. (The print can smudge.) Without removing the pins, lift a corner to see if the print has transferred: iron it hotter and harder if the transfer is not yet clear. **Note**: Some copy machines do not heat transfer. As alternatives, use commercial photocopy heat-transfer paper or trace the cameo over a light box. On cloth, Sadie Rose will face in the opposite direction because the carbon transfer is always a mirror image of the photocopy.

6. Go over the cloth portrait with a black Pigma 01 pen while the freezer paper is still attached and before appliqué and embellishment.

   Note: Words must be reversed before transferring by iron-on photocopy. Figures 39-41 include calligraphed words in reverse, and also signature banderoles, all photocopy transfer alternatives to Sadie Rose.

Fig. 38 "Sadie Rose's Cameo" by Karan Flansha

Fig. 39 Calligraphy by Walter J. Filling (Affection, Family, Forget Me Not) reversed for right-facing photocopy transfer.

Fig. 40 Banderole from a printer's die of a calling card, found stamped on an antique Baltimore Album Quilt.

Fig. 41

"Sadie Rose" by Karan Flansha

Pattern 8 "Sadie Rose"

PROCEDURE

Karan entered this design into the 1996 Elly Sienkiewicz Appliqué Academy scholarship challenge and shares it here. All intrigues the viewer: the cameo within the reverse appliquéd heart, the pen-etched lady (her attention forever caught off-stage), the bead embroidery, the rose garland that highlights colors from the brocade-like appliqué cloth. By now you are so familiar with the process of reverse appliqué that we need simply note that Pattern 8 like Pattern 5 (both on page 111), requires that the orna-mentation on Layer A be completed before the block is basted for appliqué. Heat-Transferred Engravings (page 36) gives Sadie Rose's cameo and tells you how to prepare Layer A. After the transfer, proceed as for Pattern 5, cutting the center out of Layer B's heart, centering it over the Sadie Rose engraving, then reverse appliquéing its heart frame.

EMBELLISHMENT

Bead-embroider three seed beads to hold each heart border swag. Use Nymo thread (or waxed quilting thread) in beige, taking one stitch per bead. Finally, do the silk ribbon embroidery. The garland's lay-out is given on page 36. Its stitches are in the Embroidery Primer, pages 30-31.

LESSON 3

Seamless Appliqué ~ Serenely Simple

Teach us Delight in simple things, and Mirth that has no bitter springs.

—Rudyard Kipling, "The Children's Song"

Seamless appliqué was popular in the nineteenth century. The difference is that back then the fabric was more finely woven and its raw edge was sewn with up to forty blanket stitches per inch. Today seamless appliqué is pre-bonded to the foundation cloth, so that our stitches need only be modestly close.

Materials

For basic supplies, see Appliqué Supplies, page 12.

PATTERN 9
Appliqué (Layer A): 9" square of cotton backed with lightweight fusible bonding web
Background (Layer B): 9" square of cotton

PATTERN 10
Appliqué (Layer A): 6" scrap of cotton backed with lightweight fusible bonding web
Appliqué (Layer B): 6" scrap of cotton backed with lightweight fusible bonding web
Background (Layer C): 9" square of cotton

PATTERN 11
Appliqué (Layer A): Two 7" scraps of cotton "pieced" together in the process of being ironed onto the fusible bonding web (taught on page 40)
Background (Layer B): 9" square of cotton

Supplies for Embellishment

PATTERN 9
Antique gold embroidery thread and golden yellow silk buttonhole twist (both for blanket stitch); metallic gold sewing thread (for top stitching leaves); 50 weight silk thread (for thread fern).

PATTERNS 9, 10, AND 11
Variegated 4mm and 7mm silk embroidery ribbon for French knots and tendrils; silk buttonhole twist for crewel and blanket stitch; cotton floss for stems and French knots.

Beatific Buttonhole Stitch

The *Victorian Encyclopedia of Needlework* notes that chintz cut-outs were glued (and includes the recipe!) to the background fabric, then edge-finished by "button hole" stitching. The *Encyclopedia* defines the buttonhole stitch as "close blanket-stitching." A compilation of modern sources distinguishes those stitches, broadening our choices for edge stitching seamless appliqué.

The Blanket Stitch

Work toward yourself, taking a small needle bite by entering the background (Layer B) from inside the appliqué (Layer A), going directly into and under Layer B, and coming up through it just outside Layer A. Pass the needle over the tail of the thread as shown below. Hold the tension by pressing your left thumb over the tail until the finishing pull. The beauty of the stitch is always in the rhythm set up by evenness of length and depth.

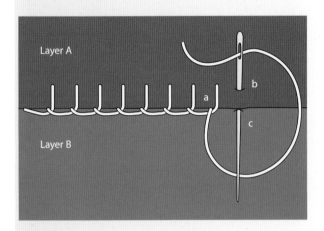

The Tailor's Buttonhole Stitch

This stitch is worked away from you. The thread is looped and the needle pulled through it—first to the left, then to the right—to lie as a protective ridge along the cut edge.

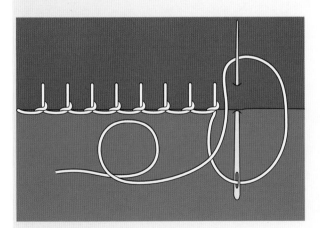

Back-to-Back Blanket Stitch (Thread Fern)

Work the right side toward yourself. At the outer tip, reverse the direction of the cloth so that you work the left side toward yourself as well.

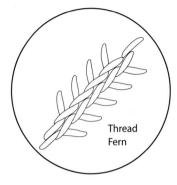

Back-to-Back Blanket Stitch

Triangular Blanket Stitch

Also called closed blanket stitch; pairs of stitch legs lean to touch each other, enclosing a triangle.

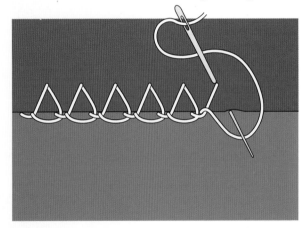

Beaded Blanket Stitch

Scoop the bead up on a milliners needle at (c), reinsert the needle beneath the bead, then come up to begin a new stitch at (a), two threads to the right of (c).

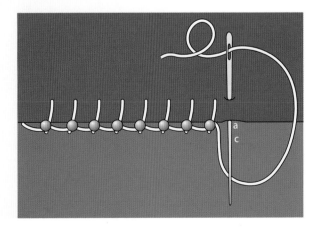

Bonding Web Basics

What is bonding web? Bonding web is perforated plastic film which, when ironed between two cloths, bonds them together. Innovations include a temporary protective paper backing; different weights for different duties; and, most recently (on Steam-a-Seam™), repositionable adhesive on one or both sides to aid design. For cotton quiltmaking, use light- or regular weight. Either one virtually eliminates the need for an embroidery hoop because it stiffens the fabric and holds it taut. Steam-a-Seam's repositionable adherence is wonderful, but it can be hard to needle by hand. Wonder Under™ and Aleene's Hot Stitch® are excellent for handwork. While basics follow, always read the manufacturer's directions:

Method A: This method avoids reversal problems with asymmetrical patterns. Iron the fusible bonding to the fabric's wrong side. Mark the cloth's right side with the appliqué template, then pick up the following instructions at Step 3.

Method B: By this method, the pattern is transferred as a mirror image at the same time as the bonding web is applied to the fabric:

1. Cut the web swatch a bit larger than the template. Trace the template (here, Pattern 9 from page 112) onto the web's paper side.
2. Use a hot, dry iron set on cotton. For five seconds, press the web's rough side to the cloth's wrong side. Let cool.

Pattern 9's appliqué, backed with fusible bonding web, cut out on the traced template line, and heat-bonded to background fabric.

3. With the paper still attached, cut out the fusible-backed appliqué on the drawn line, then peel off the bonding web's protective paper.
4. Position the fusible fabric shape, web side down, on the background cloth. Using a damp paper towel as a press cloth, iron the appliqué firmly for about ten seconds, or until the press cloth is dry. Let cool. Should the fusible fabric still lift, iron again, using more pressure, but do not overdo it. (If pressed with too much heat or for too long, bonding will fail.)

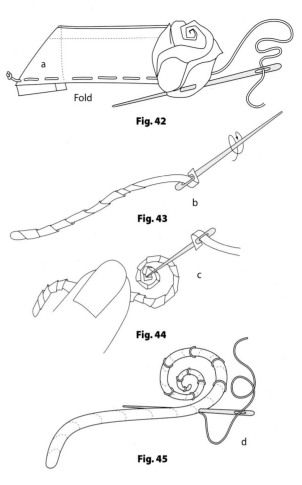

Fig. 42

Fig. 43

Fig. 44

Fig. 45

"Love Is a Rose" by Elly Sienkiewicz

Pattern 9 "Love Is a Rose"

PROCEDURE/APPLIQUÉ APPROACH

For full pattern transfer and block preparation, see Bonding Web Basics, page 40, and Adept Needleturn Appliqué, pages 14-22.

After Pattern 9 (page 112) has been bonded to the background cloth, the appliqué fun begins! The photo above shows three different gold threads used in the spacious (just under ⅛" apart) blanket stitch that finishes the edge's seamless appliqué. Both antique gold embroidery thread (single), and metallic gold sewing thread (double), outline the appliqué. The central leaf veins are top stitched in a single gold metallic thread. Fine-scale differences in thread weight vary the embroidered lines, imparting sensitivity and expressiveness like the line of a fine pencil drawing.

EMBELLISHMENT

Corsage-like, a single wire-edged ribbon rosebud rests on a cascading vine. See pattern page 112 for a full-size embellishment layout and stitch key. Embroider the rose's stem first, then the tendril stitched vine (both in Figure 45). Tack down the rose. Fill out the foliage with lazy daisy and pierced leaf stitched leaves and a spray of French knots.

Fig. 42 Pattern 9's Rose Make the rosebud from a 1½"-wide x 4½"-long cut of shaded French wired ribbon. Fold it lengthwise so that the front selvage lies ⅛" higher than the back. Bend the left end backward (**a**) and the right end forward, both at a 45° angle. Running stitch the fold from left to right, but do not cut the thread at the end.

Roll the ribbon from right to left, first tightly then looser, so that it flares out a bit. Pull the thread tightly to gather the unrolled end and finish by pulling the left end to the right and across the bud.

Stitch the base of the bud to hold its shape and secure the stitches. With tweezers, twist the center whorl clockwise and down to look like a tight bud center. Stitch the bud to the appliquéd heart.

Fig. 43 The Tendril Stitch The tendril stitched vine requires two needles: A #11 milliners needle threaded with silk 100 thread should be at the ready for couching the tendril stitch and threading through its center channel to secure its shape. Thread the second needle, a #24 chenille, with 4mm silk embroidery ribbon for the tendril stitch. Begin the stitch by piercing the background from back to front. Extending the ribbon into the air (**b**), twirl the needle clockwise between thumb and forefinger until the first 2½" or so of the ribbon is coiled. With your left hand, gently pinch the top of the twist to keep it from unwinding.

Fig. 44 Lay it on the cloth, letting the end coil like a snake. Hold it there with your thumb (**c**).

Fig. 45 Re-enter the foundation cloth, pulling the ribbon through until just the coiled ribbon rests on top. Let the needle of silk ribbon dangle beneath the foundation while with your right hand you tunnel the milliners needle through the coil (**d**), tacking and couching it to the foundation cloth.

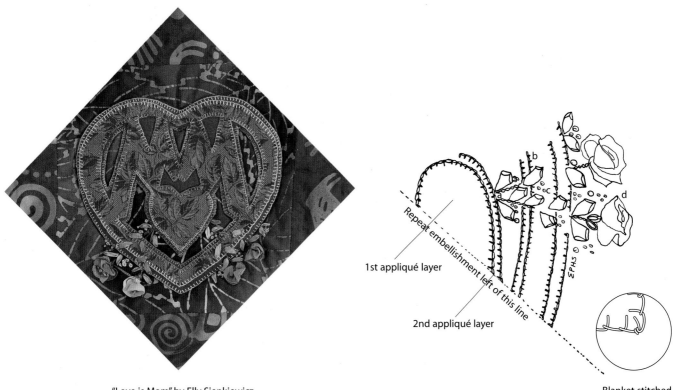

"Love is Mom" by Elly Sienkiewicz

Fig. 46 Two long-stemmed roses lie at either side of the center heart

Pattern 10 "Love is Mom"

PROCEDURE

For full details, see Appliqué Supplies, page 12.

While mothering is complex, the graphic word "Mom" is neatly symmetrical and full of design promise! In Pattern 10 (page 113), Mom is the basis for a study in echo-appliqué:

1. Pattern 10 includes a first appliqué layer (Template A), and a second appliqué layer (Template B). Trace each onto contact paper, cutting each template out double on the fold.
2. Stick Template A to fused appliqué Layer A. Cut the cloth, right at the paper's edge. Repeat for Template B.
3. Peel off the Pattern 10 templates.
4. Stack the first appliqué (A) on top of its echo (B), centering both over Layer C. Press to heat-bond the layers together and to the background.

Key: (**a**) Stem stitch (three strands cotton floss)
(**b**) Pierced leaf stitch (4mm silk embroidery ribbon)
(**c**) French knots (three strands cotton floss, others in six strands)
(**d**) Gathered and rolled silk ribbon roses (7mm silk embroidery ribbon). These roses and stitches are taught in the Embroidery Primer on pages 30-31.

APPLIQUÉ AND EMBELLISHMENT

Blanket stitch the echoed layers. (I used a #10 Richard Hemming® milliners needle and one strand of YLI's® overdyed silk floss. Two colors (#114, #157) of this floss were used, the darker one inside the heart and the lighter one on the heart's outer outline. Figure 46 shows a finishing stitch tacking the point down, then a new stitch begun at the same place, heading up the right side of the point. By contrast, when the blanket stitch is done ⅛" (or less) apart, the leg completing the stitch at the point can simply begin the stitch to the right of the point, all in one motion. Figure 46 also details Mom's embellishment.

"Love is Sis" by Elly Sienkiewicz

Pattern 11 "Love is Sis"

PROCEDURE

This block experiments with "patchworked" seamless appliqué.

1. Trace Pattern 11 (page 113) onto contact paper and cut the template out on the drawn line.

   a) To "piece" the appliqué: Lay one appliqué print scrap on top of the other, wrong sides together. With a rotary cutter and ruler, slice a shared straight edge through the two layers.

   b) Flop the top print over so that the two lie side-by-side, clean-cut edges abutting and wrong sides up.

   c) Position a 6" scrap of fusible bonding web, web side to the paired cloths' wrong sides, and iron it to "piece" the appliqué scraps.

2. Finger-press the paper template to the right side of the pieced cloth, positioning it so that both appliqué prints show.

3. Cut out Pattern 11 around the template, peel off the fusible web's paper backing, and heat-bond the pieced appliqué to the foundation cloth.

4. Using two strands of silk or cotton embroidery floss, blanket stitch the appliqué. (Stitching the patchwork "seams" is optional.) The embellishment layout and key is given beside the pattern on page 113. Its simple loop-stitched silk ribbon flowers and other stitches are taught on pages 30-31.

And all the loveliest things there be
Come so simply, so, it seems to me.

—Edna St. Vincent Millay, "The Goose Girl"

LESSON 4

Lacework, etc.~ Elegant Capers in Cloth

"Dr. Spock…warned that you should never startle a baby with something shockingly new: babies like a toy that is very much like the last one, only slightly different. I thought this was a profound insight into human taste in general. When something is new, we like it also to be familiar. In this way, women might be even more conservative than men."

—Danielle Crittenden, *What Does Woman Want?*, National Review

We grasp mirror images quickly. Even fresh with surprise, such a design comforts us by its order and stability. From childhood's valentines, we remember papercutting, so add familiarity to that art's appeal. Lace-like appliqués and lace itself are elegant touches and essential characters in our fancywork pantheon.

Materials

For basic supplies, see Appliqué Supplies, page 12.

PATTERN 12
Appliqué (Layer A): 7" scrap of ecru tone-on-tone cotton print
Background (Layer B): 9" square of dark cotton print

PATTERN 13
Appliqué (Layer A): 7" square of cotton print
Background (Layer B): 9" square of cotton solid

PATTERN 14
Appliqué (Layer A): 9" square of medium dark cotton print
Background (Layer B): 9" square of light cotton print

PATTERN 15
Appliqué (Layer A): 7" scrap of white lace, 18" premade white singlefold bias tape (½" wide)
Background (Layer B): 9" square of dark cotton solid

Supplies for Embellishment

PATTERN 12
White cotton floss; 4mm silk embroidery ribbon; silk buttonhole twist; French shaded wired ribbon scraps for flora.

PATTERN 13
Silk buttonhole twist for crewel stitch edge-embroidery

PATTERN 14
6" scrap of cotton print for leaves; gold metallic thread for top stitch, ¼"-wide satin ribbon, seed beads or 4mm silk embroidery ribbon for French knots; silk buttonhole twist for stems; French shaded wired ribbon scraps for flora.

PATTERN 15
7mm silk embroidery ribbon for loop flowers, 4mm silk embroidery ribbon for fern; French shaded wired ribbon scraps for flora.

"Filigreed Heart" by Susan Gilbert

Pattern 12 "Filigreed Heart"

PROCEDURE

For full instructions, see Block Preparation and Pattern Transfer, page 110.

What an utterly ladylike papercut heart! If designing mirror-image appliqués appeals to you, see *Papercuts and Plenty* for a wealth of pattern-making formulas. Pattern 12 is done by seamless appliqué. Gown this heart in the look of pale lace, then pin roses and baby's breath to her shoulder. Trace Pattern 12 (page 114) onto fusible web, turning it into a seamless appliqué (as taught on page 40), heat-bonded to the background cloth.

APPLIQUÉ APPROACH

Blanket-stitch (page 39) the fused appliqué with a strand of white embroidery floss to enhance the lace-like look. Sulky® machine embroidery thread could be used; it has a sheen and gives an antique look when combined with finer stitches.

EMBELLISHMENT

Make a corsage including three rolled roses. Make the first from a ⅞" x 18" length of shaded wired ribbon following Steps 1-7. In addition, make two smaller roses (the diameter of a quarter coin), each from a ⅞" x 9" length.

1. U-turn gather the ribbon using the bottom wire, pulling the ribbon down to expose 2" of wire on both ends simultaneously (a).
2. Roll each wire around a toothpick to knot it (b).
3. Twist the first inch of the ribbon's length into a stem (c).

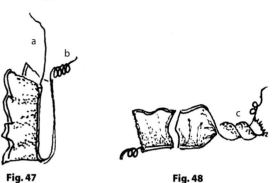

Fig. 47   **Fig. 48**

4. Holding the stem up in the air (d), roll the gathered ribbon concentrically around it loosely.
5. When the rose's base is 1½" in diameter, fold the remaining raw edge (e) in toward the center.
6. Slip two long pins under the gathered edge, pin-basting the rose in an "X."

Fig. 49 A gathered and rolled wire-edged ribbon rose

7. Flatten the stem beneath the rose and arrange the flower's petals from the right side. Use tweezers to twist the center whorl tightly, arranging the rose into some pleasing visage, like that in Figure 50's corsage layout.

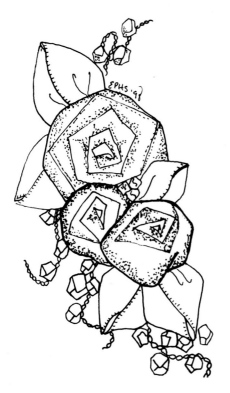

Fig. 50 Pattern 12's corsage layout of roses and baby's breath

Make five twisted leaves (two larger leaves from a 1½" x 5" length of wired ribbon and three smaller leaves from a ⅞" x 3" length).

1. Fold the ribbon halves straight down from the top center edge to form a prairie point (f).
2. Twist the tail-ends together (g) one full turn to hold the leaf's shape.

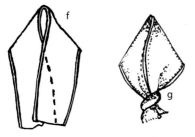

Fig. 51 A twisted leaf

Assemble the Corsage

1. Pin the larger rose over the larger leaves and the smaller roses over the smaller leaves, as pictured. Using matching thread and the tack or stab stitch, sew their outside edges securely to the block.
2. With silk buttonhole thread, crewel stitch (page 26) the baby's breath stems, then punctuate them with French knot blossoms (page 31) in 4mm silk embroidery ribbon.

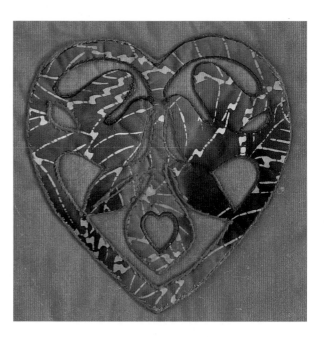

"Doves in Love" by Elly Sienkiewicz

Pattern 13 "Doves in Love"

PROCEDURE

For full instructions, see Block Preparation and Pattern Transfer, page 110.

A flowing papercut design, "Doves in Love's" familiar heart-shape perimeter signals the perfect warm-up starting place for cutaway appliqué. But the heart's interior—its tight inside corners and sharp points—will test your skills! Thread a #11 milliners needle with 100 weight neutral silk thread and think miniature—even though this design plays a wide range on the size scale.

1. Trace Pattern 13 (page 114) onto contact paper.
2. Cut out the template so that no drawn line remains.
3. Press the template firmly (vertical axis on grain) onto the appliqué cloth, Layer A. Place Layer A over Layer B, right sides up. Pin the four corners and center from the back. Put three small pins (through the template and both fabric layers) near where the appliqué will start. Move these pins as the appliqué progresses, keeping them in the vicinity of the stitching.

APPLIQUÉ APPROACH

For full instructions, see Adept Needleturn Appliqué, pages 14–22.

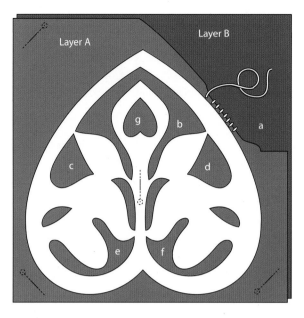

Fig. 52 Pattern 13 by cutaway needleturn appliqué

"Hand-Held Heart" by Trevian Connor

4. Hold the heart point up as in Figure 52. Cut the seam ³⁄₁₆" wide on the side and a full ¼" at the outside point. Appliqué the heart's point, curves, and corner according to the directions on pages 14 to 22.

5. Begin at (a) and stitch counterclockwise around the heart. Try sewing close to the paper on this block, holding your work so that you are looking down into the needleturned fold, rather than over it. (Envision holding half of a peanut butter sandwich and looking directly into the peanut butter. The bread slices are the template paper above and the background cloth below. The peanut butter is the seam's fold through which you stitch.) The paper template should function as a third hand, making fine appliqué easier to do. But if it frustrates you, draw around the template with a black Pigma Micron 01 pen, then remove the template. Your way is the best way!

6. Letters (b) through (g) simply suggest a sequence for sewing the larger interior spaces first, then the smaller ones.

7. When the needleturn is done, crewel stitch the appliqué's outline with silk buttonhole twist. Follow the same stitching order as you did for the appliqué.

8. Refer to crewel stitch instructions on page 26 and perfect your lassoed corners and fly-stitched points. (This embellishment is shown as a close-up detail on the pattern page.)

Pattern 14 "Hand-Held Heart"

PROCEDURE
For full instructions, see Block Preparation and Pattern Transfer, page 110, and review Cutaway Appliqué and Needleturn in Motion, pages 15-22.

With lessons to teach, this appliqué papercut has American folk art precedents both in its jagged border and in the heart and hands motif. Trevian sweeps that homey nineteenth century heritage forward to the twenty-first with her bead-stitched ribbon banner and floral ribbon cockade.

1. Trace Pattern 14 (page 115) onto contact paper.

2. When cut, press the template to the appliqué cloth (Layer A) and pin Layer A to Layer B (right sides up). Then big-stitch baste, ½" outside the heart, through the paper template and the cloth layers. Big-stitch baste inside the center heart and hands, too.

APPLIQUÉ APPROACH
For full instructions, see Adept Needleturn Appliqué, pages 14-22.

We are still in the land of the Lilliputians with this block, so hike forward with the finest milliners needle and silk or cotton machine embroidery thread you've got on hand! Hold the block with the heart point up (as in Figure 52). Right-handers start the cutaway needleturn appliqué on the right-hand straight of the small center heart. After you have navigated the point, a tiny hand beckons. The path down into the valley of the thumb and forefinger is a familiar inside/outside point, though a bit treacherous. After cresting the thumb, there is a brief respite before two sharp inner corners signal the beginning of a picket fence of points. (In classic appliqué this is called a dogtooth triangle border.) Climbing this pattern's multiple peaks can only get easier, for there is a trick to it:

1. Cut 2" of Layer A, a solid ⅛" above and parallel to the row of points as shown in Figure 53's detail.

2. Cut into the first six valleys, giving adjacent mountainsides equal seam allowance and stopping each cut three threads short of the template.

3. Needleturn the full triangle seam under the adjacent mountain. Reread how to needleturn inside and outside points (pages 17-19), then seek the bliss of mastery!

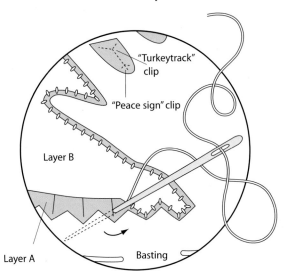

Fig. 53 Detail: Needleturning Pattern 14's picket fence points

4. When the block's southern mountain range is behind you, venture again to the isthmus of "Heart and Hands." Complete its lower border and then its upper boundaries (including the jagged heart top (a), after which you will sail the rim of Valentine Lake (b) and portage to the smaller finger lakes (c).

5. Lest you get lost in (c)'s narrow waterways, cut each seam allowance into a peace sign, as shown in Figure 53's detail. For greater freedom, draw (b) and (c)'s outlines in Pigma Micron 01 pen

and dispose of the paper template. When you've become fond of this small world, which at first seemed so foreign and formidable, leave a monument to your visit: a gay ribbon in blue for the soul, and a rose for love.

Fig. 54 Pattern 14, "Hand-held Heart" with embellishment details

EMBELLISHMENT

6. Drape the satin ribbon (¼" x 9") and tack it in place with seed bead embroidery (B).

7. Pin two scraps, right-sides together, then draw Pattern 14's Template A (page 115) twice, leaving ½" between them for the two leaves' seam allowances.

8. For each leaf: Running stitch (or machine straight stitch) the seam, then slit the back layer and turn the leaf right-sides out.

9. Top stitch the leaves to Layer A, over the heart, sew veins into the leaves at the same time.

10. Fashion the rolled rose (Figures 47-49) from ⅞" x 12" of shaded wired ribbon gathered, then rolled around a ⅞" x 5" length of a shade darker ribbon pinched into shape. Stitch the rose (C) over the leaves as shown in Figure 54.

"Roses of My Heart" by Janet Cochran

Pattern 15 "Roses of My Heart"

PROCEDURE

For full instructions, see Block Preparation and Pattern Transfer, page 110.

Fancy appliqué can be more clever than complex, as Janet's use of lace and ribbon proves.

1. Pattern 15 uses Pattern 7's (page 111) template. Cut that template out of contact paper.
2. Draw the template's outline onto Layer B with a Pigma Micron 01 pen.
3. Next, use the template to cut a heart of the same size in Layer A's lace. Gently remove the contact paper and pin, then big-stitch baste the lace to the line drawn on the background.

APPLIQUÉ APPROACH

4. Iron open lightly, one fold of the 18" length of the bias so that you can still see the crease line.
5. Pin one end of the bias (open fold-side up), extending ¾" into the top center of the heart (a).
6. Pin the bias-cut edge on the drawn line, with the fold facing the heart's center (b).

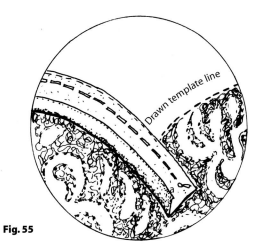

Fig. 55

7. Running stitch the crease line, from top center counterclockwise and back to top center. Refold the bias at (a) before you overlap the finishing tail (c). Trim excess bias at (d), leaving a 1" tail.

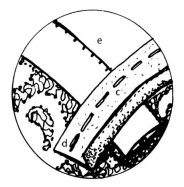

Fig. 56 Finishing the bias frame

8. Appliqué the bias to the heart's perimeter, using the tack stitch (or, for speed, the invisible running stitch, page 14).
9. At the heart's outside point, appliqué a pleat to eliminate the excess. At the inside corner, the finishing edge crosses over the starting edge. All this will be hidden by the flowers.

EMBELLISHMENT

The heart's floral swag includes the following elements:

A. Two rolled roses (page 45), each made from a ⅞" x 9" length of shaded wired ribbon.

B. Three seamed leaves and six tulip petals, each made the same way (Figure 57) from a ⅞" x 6" length of shaded wired ribbon.

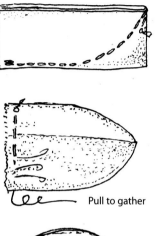

Pull to gather

Fig. 57 Seamed leaf (B)

C. Eight five-petaled flowers fashioned from 7mm silk embroidery ribbon are looped and sewn by the pierced leaf stitch (page 31), then filled with three-strand cotton floss French knots.

Fig. 58 Loop stitched flower variation

D. Half a dozen complex fronds of maidenhair fern, pierced leaf stitched in 4mm silk ribbon (page 30).

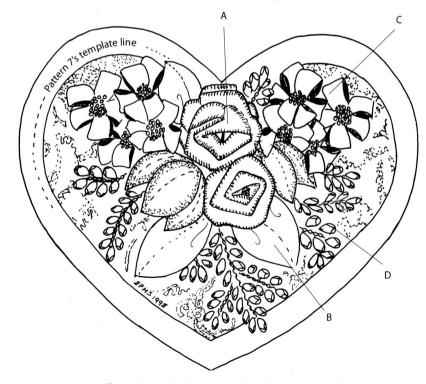

Fig. 59 Pattern 15, "Roses of My Heart" floral layout

LESSON 5

Ultra-Simple UltraSuede® Appliqué

Perfect simplicity is unconsciously audacious.

—George Meredith

UltraSuede needs no seam turned under, has an inviting texture and nifty colors, and is easily sewn. This lesson's dynamic block patterns could alternatively be made from cotton. With seams to turn under, and tight curves and corners to control, their mastery in cotton would be fancy appliqué indeed!

Materials

For basic supplies, see Appliqué Supplies, page 12.

PATTERN 16
Appliqué (Layer A): 7" scrap of UltraSuede
Background (Layer B): 9" square of cotton print

PATTERN 17
Appliqué (Layer A): 5" scrap of UltraSuede
Background (Layer B): 9" square of cotton print

PATTERN 18
Appliqué (Layer A): Scraps of UltraSuede in gray, black, white, greens, reds, roses, and pinks
Oval appliqué: 8" scrap of fusible-backed variegated sky blue
Background (Layer B): 9" square of cotton print

PATTERN 19
UltraSuede appliqués: Scraps of black, greens, reds, roses, and pinks
Oval appliqué: 8" scrap of fusible-backed variegated sky blue
Background: 9" square of cotton print

PATTERN 20
UltraSuede appliqués: Scraps of off-whites, greens, reds, and roses
Oval appliqué: 8" scrap of fusible-backed variegated sky blue
Background: 9" square of cotton print

PATTERN 21
UltraSuede appliqués: Scraps of dark maroons, greens, reds, and roses
Oval appliqué: 8" scrap of fusible-backed variegated sky blue
Background: 9" square of cotton print

Supplies for Embellishment

PATTERNS 16 TO 19 AND 21
Antique gold embroidery thread

PATTERNS 17 TO 21
4mm silk embroidery ribbon; black Pigma Micron 01 pen.

PATTERN 18
⅛" x 3" gold grosgrain ribbon; cotton or silk pale gray-green embroidery thread.

PATTERN 19
2" x 7" scrap of medium mesh waste canvas

PATTERN 20
Aquarelle or Prismacolor colored pencils; 4mm and 7mm white silk embroidery ribbon.

All About UltraSuede Appliqué

UltraSuede is synthetic leather from Springs Industries. It is easy to use and adds rich texture to your work. While expensive, only tiny amounts are needed for appliqué fancywork. Both medium- and lightweight are easily needled by hand, using a #10 Richard Hemming milliners needle (rather than a leather needle). Use a strong thread: Nymo (nylon), polyester, or silk finished cotton-covered polyester. UltraSuede can be embroidered, beaded, painted, shaded with colored pencils or Cray-Pas, glued, appliquéd in multiple layers, or embellished with a Pigma Micron pen. It is wonderful!

Which side is the wrong side? Fold the UltraSuede swatch's corner over so that you see both the upper and the underside at the same time. The right side's nap is deeper and its color more vibrant than that of the wrong side.

Which UltraSuede side gets the template?
Occasionally the paper template leaves residue. As a precaution, adhere the template to the UltraSuede's wrong side. Likewise, finger-press contact paper gently—or iron freezer paper lightly—to the Ultra-Suede. Note that template paper on the wrong side reverses the pattern when the appliqué is sewn down. Think this process through before marking the background fabric for placement. When is sticking the template to the right side of the UltraSuede preferable to sticking it to the wrong side? When the pattern's fine scale or its layering will be appliquéd more easily with paper template left on top. Make the template less tacky by adhering it to, then removing it from, a piece of cotton cloth.

PROCEDURE

1. Trace the UltraSuede appliqué's pattern to contact or freezer paper.
2. With the protective paper still attached, trace the template (omitting pattern bridges) onto the background cloth with a black Pigma Micron 005 or 01 pen.
3. Next, finger-press the contact paper template to the wrong side of the UltraSuede.
4. Cut out the appliqué along the paper's edge. Add no seam allowance. The exception is to add an ⅛" layering allowance to the bottom layer when it lies under another appliqué.

5. Smear the back of small to medium UltraSuede appliqués with gluestick to baste them to the background cloth. For larger appliqués, apply the gluestick to the background cloth inside the drawn pattern shape. Avoid getting glue on the right side of the UltraSuede, where it will dry shiny.
6. To appliqué UltraSuede, use a strong matching thread and the decorative crewel (page 26) or blanket stitch (page 39). Alternatively, use a non-decorative stitch like the tack stitch (page 13). Take each stitch into and out of the drawn outline for precise alignment. While this stitch shows very little, it pulls the cut edge down, sloping it toward the background. At ten stitches to the inch this appliqué looks utterly elegant! Two other non-decorative stitches that work well with UltraSuede follow.

NON-DECORATIVE ULTRASUEDE STITCHES

The Hawaiian tack stitch rises from under the background cloth, brushes the UltraSuede's outside edge, then (ideally as a second motion) pierces downward through the UltraSuede and the background, opposite where it arose, just a needle's width inside the edge. The Hawaiian tack stitch helps control a thicker appliqué like UltraSuede or velvet.

The pick stitch. Perhaps you have put a zipper in by hand using a pick stitch. A pick stitch cannot be seen from the top of the appliqué, for it progresses along the underside of the background, reaching up at close, regular intervals to pick up a tiny bit of the UltraSuede and stitch it to the background. The pick stitch is worked just inside the cut edge. It is strong, but the tack stitch is stronger. Use the pick stitch for effect, when leaving the cut suede cloth's edge crisp is a design advantage.

"Inseparable" by Elly Sienkiewicz

Pattern 16 "Inseparable"

PROCEDURE/APPLIQUÉ

For full instructions, see Block Preparation and Pattern Transfer, page 110, and All About UltraSuede Appliqué, page 52.

1. Use Pattern 16 (page 115) to make contact paper templates. While the protective paper is still attached, trace around the template to transfer the pattern (exclusive of paper bridge) to the background cloth.

2. This lacy template would be hard to handle if the protective backing were removed all at once; therefore first remove the right half's protection, finger-pressing the template's right side to the UltraSuede's wrong side. Repeat on the left.

3. Cut out the UltraSuede appliqué (including the bridges) along the contact paper's edge.

4. Remove the entire contact paper template.

5. Dab gluestick carefully on the background within the drawn pattern shape.

6. Place the UltraSuede appliqué over the background, again finger-pressing the right side, then the left side.

7. Clip off the pattern bridges.

8. Use a non-decorative stitch (page 52) to sew the edges of the UltraSuede appliqués.

EMBELLISHMENT

Embroider the already appliquéd edge by crewel stitch (page 26) using antique gold embroidery thread. (See illustration on page 115.) With the same thread, stitch a French knot eye for each dove. On the other hand, if the challenge of doing the appliqué with embroidery thread and the crewel stitch appeals to you, this is the ideal place to skip Step 8's non-decorative appliqué and do it as part of the embellishment. With no seams to turn under, you can perfect catching a needle's width bite of the UltraSuede each time you take the emerging part of the crewel stitch.

"Love in Bloom" by Rosalie Schmidt

Pattern 17 "Love in Bloom"

PROCEDURE/APPLIQUÉ

For full instructions, see Block Preparation and Pattern Transfer, page 110.

1. Trace Pattern 17 (page 116) onto contact paper. Include the pattern bridges, but omit the silk ribbon embroidery.
2. Proceed as for Pattern 16: outline the appliqué (without the pattern bridges) on the background.
3. Finger-press the template to the UltraSuede's right side. Cut out the UltraSuede appliqué.
4. Appliqué the letters down finely, cutting off each pattern bridge as you come to it.

EMBELLISHMENT

4. Pattern 17's silk ribbon embroidery is diagrammed on page 116 in the Pattern Section. Pencil the rose stem's center onto the background cloth. Think of it as a curvaceous "Y" when drawing it by eye. Draw a ⅛" dot for each rose and bud.
5. Use green 4mm silk embroidery ribbon for the leaves and calyxes (a) in pierced leaf stitch, and for the stems (c) in back stitch. Use pink and cream 4mm silk embroidery ribbons for the buds (b) in lazy daisy stitch, and for the spiral roses (d). While the back stitch is taught on the pattern, the other stitches are taught in the Embroidery Primer on pages 30-31.

The Oval Wreaths of Fancy Sampler Album II

Oval wreaths, a-dance with hearts and leaves, frame Patterns 18 to 21. Such a wreath could cradle words, drawings, or sundry appliqués. What objects hold your memories? A canoe? A cottage? Or what creatures? A cat? A crustacean? Patterns 18 to 21 feature simple UltraSuede shapes each held by an oval frame made thus:

1. Trace (with black Pigma Micron 01 pen) Pattern 18's (page 117) oval center, embroidered wreath stem line, and appliquéd heart/leaf frame onto the 9" background square.
2. Heat-bond the sky blue oval, centered, onto the background square.
3. With a black Pigma Micron 01 pen, outline the oval's interior appliqué, depending on which pattern will fill the wreath.
4. Appliqué the frame of UltraSuede hearts and UltraSuede leaves, having first outlined, then gluesticked the appliqués in place.
5. Embellish the hearts with three antique gold embroidery thread long-stemmed French knots each. With the same thread, crewel stitch outline the large front center heart, then inscribe it using a Pigma Micron 01 pen.
6. Embroider the wreath's two stems: the outer one in antique gold crewel stitch and the inner one in three strands of cotton or silk (pale gray-green) by chain stitch.
7. With a #22-#24 chenille needle and variegated 4mm silk embroidery ribbon, add leaves to the stem by pierced leaf stitch (page 30) taken at a diagonal, stitching the inside leaves, then the outside ones. Skip where interior appliqué (Patterns 18, 20, 21) will interrupt the wreath.
8. After completing the leaf wreath, finish it according to each pattern's directions.

"I Thee Wed" by Elly Sienkiewicz

Pattern 18 "I Thee Wed"

PROCEDURE/APPLIQUÉ/EMBELLISHMENT

For full instruction, read All About UltraSuede Appliqué, page 52, and The Oval Wreaths, page 54.
As part of making the oval wreath, draw Pattern 18's (page 117) appliqués onto the blue oval as suggested, then proceed. In the glue-basting process, "I Thee Wed" uses abutted appliqué: the shapes are fitted right next to each other like pieces in a wooden jigsaw puzzle. Just one appliqué needs layering: The gold wedding bands (each ⅛" x ½" of grosgrain ribbon) must be glued around the appropriate fingers before the hands are glue-basted to the foundation cloth. The appliqués are tack stitched except for the visibly decorative blanket stitching of the cuffs. Each hand reaches for a heart outlined in antique gold crewel stitch and sprouting three long-stemmed French knots.

Heart and leaf appliqués

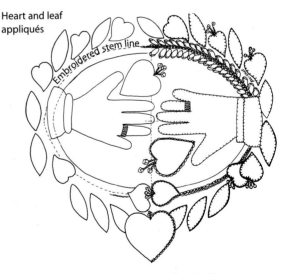

Fig. 60 Pattern 18, "I Thee Wed"

"Call Me Quiltmaker" by Elly Sienkiewicz

Fig. 61 Pattern 19 "Call Me Quiltmaker"

Pattern 19 "Call Me Quiltmaker"

PROCEDURE/APPLIQUÉ/EMBELLISHMENT

For full instruction, read All About UltraSuede Appliqué, page 52, and The Oval Wreaths, page 54.
The words "call me a quilter" inspired this block. "Fiber Artist" may sound more elevated to some, but to me, the nomen *Quiltmaker* stands more for what I value most: an honorable and steadfast person, one whose fellowship fills me with gratitude. The charted alphabet on page 118 invites you to wear your heart—by any name—on a Fancy Sampler block! To make this one, draw Pattern 19's (page 118) appliqués onto the blue background as part of constructing the oval wreath, then proceed by appliquéing the UltraSuede tree. Next gluestick down the UltraSuede circle overlays, embroidering these 1930s roses with three or four overlapping straight stitches in 4mm silk ribbon. Pull the silk ribbon around the spherical shapes with fine silk thread tack stitches. The leaves are pierced leaf stitched 4mm silk embroidery ribbon (page 30). The cross stitch was done using waste canvas. After signing and dating the block in Pigma Micron pen, ironing as suggested on page 13 will finish this block nicely.

How to use Waste Canvas

Waste canvas is available at stitchery shops and was used to do the cross stitch in Pattern 19. Waste canvas is thread woven like graph paper with an easily needled hole in the center of each square. The canvas is heavily starched to guide the cross stitch. Pin, then baste a swatch of waste canvas in place over the UltraSuede tree. Use a #26 chenille needle and a double strand of antique gold embroidery thread. Figure 62's detail shows the cross stitch being done as a separate stitch in A. In B, all the lower stitches are done first, then the top stitch is worked over them. The top stitch should always run in the same direction. A full cross stitch alphabet is given on page 118. When the cross stitch is completed, cut the canvas between the letters, dampen the embroidery with a wet sponge, and remove ("waste") each canvas thread with tweezers.

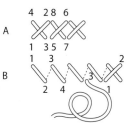

Fig. 62 Cross Stitch, Worked Two Ways

"Lovey Dovey" by Elly Sienkiewicz

Pattern 20 "Lovey Dovey"

PROCEDURE/APPLIQUÉ

For full instruction, read All About UltraSuede Appliqué, page 52, and The Oval Wreaths, page 54.
Use Pattern 20's (page 119) heart and dove templates, cut out of contact paper, to mark the blue background oval for placement. Then:

1. Cut the heart and dove appliqués from Ultra-Suede. Cut the body, legs, and beak as one templated piece. Remember to leave ⅛" layering seam on the body where the wings overlap it. Carefully remove the contact paper template.

2. Use the wing templates to cut separate wings, adding a layering seam to the right wing. Appliquéing the body and wing shapes separately sculpts them.

3. Use the body template to cut a batting insert out of thin cotton batt. Remove the template and cut the body's batting insert down by ⅛" all around. (Yes! This does cut off the beak and legs.) Gluestick the batting insert to the background to lightly pad the bird's shape.

4. Gluestick the dove appliqués to the background, over the batting.

5. With fine silk, tack stitch each appliqué to the background along its drawn outline.

Fig. 63 Pattern 20's dove sports silk ribbon embroidered feathers, inkwork, and colored pencil shadows.

EMBELLISHMENT

6. Cut the dove templates apart further, using them to pencil in (no inking for now!) the lines that separate the shoulders from the wing feathers and the body from the tail feathers. Figure 63 illustrates how these lines guide the feather embroidery.

7. **Under feathers**: With a #24 chenille needle and 4mm silk ribbon, embroider the bottom layer of tail and wing feathers from the drawn line to just beyond the UltraSuede, using the pierced leaf stitch (page 30).

8. **Upper feathers**: With a #22 chenille needle and 7mm silk ribbon, embroider the upper tail and wing feathers to cover the first third of the previously stitched feathers.

9. **Draw the bird's features,** cutting the paper templates further apart as needed to lightly draw (with a fine mechanical pencil) the eye, beak, thighs, and legs.

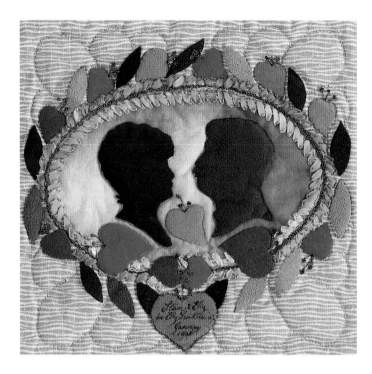

"Thirty Years Married" by Elly Sienkiewicz

10. **Stitch the eyes** with an antique gold embroidery thread French knot. Crewel stitch outline the hearts in this same gold. Place three long-stemmed French knots (crowned by a total of three French knots) emerging from the center of each heart.

11. **Colored pencil shading**: With the edges of well-sharpened colored pencils (yellow, blue, pink, and brown) shade the bird, darkening the off-white UltraSuede closest to the appliqué's drawn outline.

12. **After the birds are fully appliquéd**, embroidered, and shaded (so that smudging is no longer an issue), outline each bird in black Pigma Micron 01 pen. Draw the wrinkles on the legs and the details of the beak. Put a fine press cloth (or facial tissue) over the block and lightly dry heat-set the ink from the front. Further ironing from the back gives the silk ribbon embroidery more of a vintage look. Touch up the colored pencil shading if needed.

Pattern 21 "Thirty Years Married"

PROCEDURE

For full instruction, read All About UltraSuede Appliqué, page 52, and The Oval Wreaths, page 54. Pattern 21 (page 119) is included for size and placement of UltraSuede silhouettes—not because you'll want this pair of folks (my husband and me) in your quilt. Silhouette portraits are quilt-perfect and easy enough for anyone you wish to portray. The woman's contact paper template was placed on the wrong side, so that the finished appliqué features the UltraSuede right-side up. The opposite was done on the man, so that the finished appliqué's UltraSuede is wrong-side up. Just as with cotton prints, using both the back and the front in the same piece gives us subtle plays of color and light. To take a silhouette photograph, the subject should stand perpendicular to a blank wall, with shoulder touching the wall. Their head should fill the camera's viewer. When the picture is developed, photocopy it. Trace the appliqué templates off the photocopied photo.

LESSON 6

Wreaths ~ Set Free!

"Let me twine a wreath for thee, sacred to love and to memory."

—Inscribed on an antique Baltimore Album Quilt block

Wreaths can frame the focal point, or can be the focal point themselves. Eternally enticing, the celebratory wreath is an ancient invitation to fancywork. Both traditional wreath approaches and chirpy new ones people this lesson. In Fancy Sampler Quilt II, pictured on page 11, all blocks but the center square occur in matched frame sets of four (circles, ovals, diamonds, and heart cabochons). Each frame—and more—will be taught by book's end!

Materials

For basic supplies, see Appliqué Supplies, page 12.

PATTERN 22
Appliqué (Layer A): 8" scrap of a pictorial print
18" of singlefold ½"-wide bias made with a bias tape maker
Background (Layer B): 9" square of cotton print

PATTERN 23
Appliqué (Layer A): Approximately one yard of cotton bias made with ⅛"-wide Bias Bars by Heirloom Stitches (see Sources, page 140)
Background (Layer B): 9" square of cotton print

PATTERN 24
UltraSuede appliqués: Scraps of white, brown, flesh, purples, roses, and pinks
Sky blue circle appliqué: 6" scrap of fusible-backed variegated sky blue
Background: 9" square of cotton print

PATTERN 25
UltraSuede appliqués: Scraps of black, brown, flesh, purples, and rose
The sky blue circle appliqué: 6" scrap of fusible-backed variegated sky blue
Background: 9" square of cotton print

PATTERN 26
UltraSuede appliqués: Scraps of brown, flesh, blues, purples, and rose
Sky blue circle appliqué: 6" scrap of fusible-backed variegated sky blue
Background: 9" square of cotton print

PATTERN 27
UltraSuede appliqués: Scraps of gold and pinks
Sky blue circle appliqué: 6" scrap of fusible-backed variegated sky blue
Background: 9" square of cotton print

Supplies for Embellishment

PATTERN 22
Cotton embroidery floss; 4mm silk embroidery ribbon; variegated pearl cotton (size 5).

PATTERN 23
Sizes 3 and 5 pearl cotton; golden embroidery floss; red, salmon, and yellow 4mm silk embroidery ribbon.

PATTERNS 24 TO 27
UltraSuede scraps for the appliqué; antique gold embroidery thread; variegated 4mm silk embroidery ribbon; black Pigma Micron 01 pen.

PATTERN 24

18" antique gold braid; variegated pearl cotton (size 8 for branches, size 5 for the frame).

PATTERNS 25, 26, AND 27

Variegated pearl cotton (sizes 3, 5, and 8); variegated cotton, rayon, or wool floss for the branches; garnet beads.

PATTERN 25

18" of 3mm-wide yellow picot-edged braid

PATTERN 26

Bluebird: 4mm and 7mm silk ribbon, shaded rayon ribbon for breast

PATTERN 27

18" of Mokuba 2mm gold (#14) woven braid; 18" of 2mm yellow soutache braid; variegated 7mm silk embroidery ribbon for wings and some leaves; YLI silk embroidery floss, overdyed pearl cotton (size 5), and antique gold embroidery thread for hair; black Pigma Micron 005 pen; colored pencils.

Bias Wreath Stems

How is a wreath begun? Some, like those in Pattern 22 and the Cameo Portraits (Patterns 24 to 27), trim and embroider a fabric shape. Some, like Pattern 23, "Heart Trellis with Roses," are most easily done by twining bias-bar stems over a drawn outline. Circular wreaths on bias-cut cotton stems dominate appliquéd wreaths, yet marrying Stem Methods #2 and #3, below, to Artemis bias-cut silk ribbon (see Sources, page 140) will set your wreaths free! Three super stem-making methods, for silk or for cotton, follow.

Stem Method 1: Bias Tape Making

Begin ½"-wide (finished) bias tape with a 1"-wide strip of bias-cut cloth. Manufactured bias tape makers fold the strip as it is pressed under an iron. Figure 64 shows how our great-grandmothers did the same thing simply by using two 1½" long safety pins:

1. Pin in and out of the ironing board cover to make a tunnel (a little wider than ½"). Similarly, insert a second safety pin 2" to the right of the first.
2. Finger-press ¼" folds on either side of the 1" wide bias strip to thread it through both pins' tunnels, from left to right. Use spray starch to hold a sharper crease.

3. Hold an iron just beyond the right pin. Press the folded bias as you pull it to the right.
   Note: To sew a bias strip full circle for a wreath, abut its raw-edged ends under an appliqué. Or, plug and socket style, insert a flat end into an end folded ¼" under.

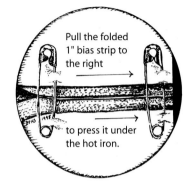

Pull the folded 1" bias strip to the right

to press it under the hot iron.

Fig. 64 Stem Method 1: Basic Bias Tape Maker

Stem Method 2: Single Drawn Stem

1. Draw a single line onto the background. (This line would mark the left side of a vertical stem, or the outside of a circular wreath.)
2. For a ¼"-wide stem: Fold a 1"-wide strip of bias in half lengthwise, right sides out.
3. Pin the bias's raw edges touching the drawn line. (Face the fold to the right side of a vertical stem. Face the fold (Fold A) to the center of a circular wreath.)
4. Running stitch ³⁄₁₆" in from and parallel to the raw edge. (After the next step, these stitches become the right side of a stem or the inside of a wreath.)
5. Finger-press Fold A to the left and over the stitches to cover the raw edges and the drawn line. (Trim the raw edges back if they show beyond the fold.)
6. Appliqué Fold A down, over the drawn line. On a wreath, the bias fold (Fold A) stretches to cover the widest part—the outside—of the circle. A stem made by this method is self-stuffed.

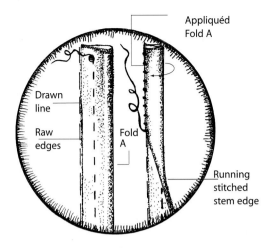

Fig. 65 Stem Method 2: Single Drawn Stem

Stem Method 3: Superfine Double-Drawn Stem

1. On background cloth, draw two stem lines ⅛" apart. (If for a circular wreath, make them concentric.) Line 1 marks the left (or outside) of the stem, line 2 marks the right (or inside) of the stem.

2. Iron a ⅝"-wide Artemis bias-cut silk ribbon in half lengthwise, right-sides out.

3. Appliqué the ribbon's fold to line 2 (see A).

4. Open the top ribbon layer (see B) and cut the bottom layer back to ¹⁄₁₆" from the appliquéd seam.

5. Needleturn the top ribbon layer under to line 1 (see C). This makes a very fine, flat, narrow stem! If you prefer to make a cotton stem, begin with a 1" wide cotton strip for ease of handling. (You will then also have to trim the top stem layer's excess to ⅜" before needleturning under to complete the stem.)

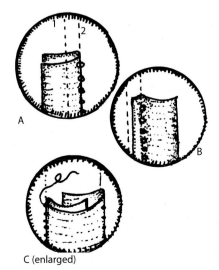

C (enlarged)

Fig. 66 Stem Method 3: Superfine Double Drawn Stem

"Home Is Where the Heart Is" by Rosalie Schmidt

Pattern 22
"Home Is Where the Heart Is"

PROCEDURE/APPLIQUÉ APPROACH

For full instructions, see Block Preparation and Pattern Transfer, page 110.

Rosalie's framed conversation print, accentuated by embroidery, is a fancywork formula full of fun!

1. Use Pattern 7 (page 111) as Pattern 22's heart: make both a contact paper template and window template. (See window template use, page 12.)

2. Move the window template until it frames an appealing motif in the pictorial print.

3. Place the adhesive-backed heart template inside that window frame and cut out the framed motif.

4. Remove the paper template and pin the printed Layer A cut-out, centered, onto the background, then apply the bias tape frame.

5. Running stitch the open fold, flip to the outside, and then appliqué the custom bias as described in Steps 4 through 9 for Pattern 15's wreath on page 49.

EMBELLISHMENT

Enjoy this block's utter freedom: freedom to find the perfect print portion and freedom to embellish it with whatever embroidery appeals to you. Rosalie used from one to three strands of cotton floss and stitches from plain to fancy. The ideal set-up for embellishing this block would be a good stitchery book and a basket of embroidery floss.

"Heart Trellis with Roses" by Laurie Toensing

Pattern 23
"Heart Trellis with Roses"

PROCEDURE/APPLIQUÉ APPROACH

For full instructions, see Block Preparation and Pattern Transfer, page 110.

Laurie's "Heart Trellis" design is joyful yet disciplined. Her model, pictured, reflects exquisite execution.

1. Mark Pattern 23's (page 120) line 1 (solid) and line 2 (dashed) on the background square with a Pigma Micron pen. Where the six small circles occur on the pattern, mark a tiny "X" on the background cloth. These show where line 2 passes under line 1. Mark the dotted embroidery line lightly in pencil.

2. To make the cotton bias, use ⅛" wide Bias Bars by Heirloom Stitches and follow the package instructions.

3. Center the prepared stem over line 1. Pin in place, then baste. Leave ½" of prepared stem hanging loose where you start at (a) and where you finish at (b). At the X-marked intersection, skip an inch of line 1's basting so that line 2's stem can be threaded underneath it.

4. Baste Line 2, second, starting with a ¼" allowance at (a) and finishing with same at (b). These excesses will be covered by the finished heart's floral corsage.

5. Tack stitch (page 13) both sides of the stems, then remove the basting. Fine thread (60 to 100 weight) and small stitches make a visible difference on these fine-scale stems!

EMBELLISHMENT

The rose vine is feather stitched in size 3 pearl cotton. A stitch diagram accompanies the pattern. Laurie notes that the buds are padded with a single straight stitch, then over-stitched with pierced leaf stitch, both in 4mm silk embroidery ribbon. The calyxes are size 5 pearl cotton, fly-stitched (page 120). The heart's corsage is illustrated on page 31. Its roses are edge-gathered 4mm silk embroidery ribbon with size 3 pearl cotton French knot centers. The side-view flowers are pierced leaf stitched with an overlay of green pierced leaf stitched calyxes, all in 4mm silk embroidery ribbon.

The Embroidered Wreaths of Fancy Sampler Quilt II

Patterns 24 to 27 are similarly framed by circular wreaths, each with minor variations. Each pattern's inner wreath is a herringbone variation embroidered between two rows of chain stitch, then couched. Within the wreath, a cameo-like oval is bounded by a fruited branch above and paired figures below. The basic approach to one of these wreathed patterns follows:

1. With a Pigma Micron 01 pen, mark Pattern 25's (page 121) sky blue circle, right-side up. Mark Lines A (the oval), B (the outer boundary of the couched herringbone frame), and C (the sky blue circle's cutting line). Mark the fruited bough's three main branches. Outline the boy and bird.

2. Cut out Pattern 25's sky blue circle, cutting a careful ⅛" beyond line C.

3. With a press cloth to protect the marking, heat-bond the sky blue circle, centered, onto the background square. Embroider the inner wreath, then the outer as described below.

4. **To begin the Couched Herringbone Wreath**, chain-stitch lines A and B in overdyed size 5 pearl cotton.

   • Aim to make line A's (the inside circle's) chain stitches a bit shorter and closer together than line B's (the outside circle's) stitches.

   • Work the herringbone stitch from left to right, coming up through line B's chain stitch at 1, re-entering through line A's chain stitch at 2, back-stitching to come up two chain stitches to its left at 3, then begin again by catching line B's third chain stitch at 4 (two links to the right of where you began at 1). Stitch in out of every third chain stitch, following Figure 68's herringbone numerical order.

   • Backstitch (in the same or a contrasting floss) to couch the herringbone. Don't embroider where interior appliqué will interrupt the wreath.

5. **The outer wreath**: Outline line B with a second row of chain stitch in size 3 pearl cotton, then a line of crewel stitched (page 26) antique gold embroidery thread. Repeat these two rows (see Figure 70) then frame the whole in 3mm yellow picot trim.

6. **The fruited bough**: Chain or crewel stitch the three main branches in two strands of overdyed cotton or silk embroidery floss, thickening them to taste (see Figure 70, d, e). Accent with antique gold crewel stitch and add fly-stitched (page 120) leaf stems. Embroider the fruit with beads, and the leaves in 4mm variegated silk embroidery ribbon, pierced leaf stitched.

The Three Stitch-Components of the Couched Herringbone Wreaths

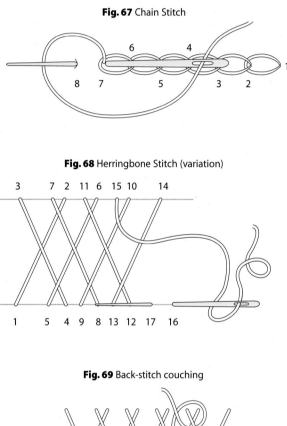

Fig. 67 Chain Stitch

Fig. 68 Herringbone Stitch (variation)

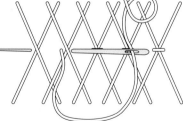

Fig. 69 Back-stitch couching

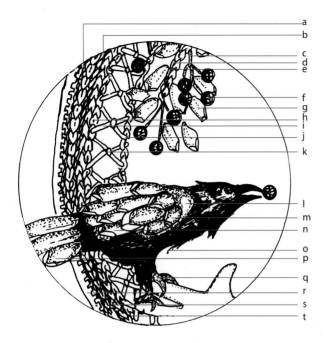

a
b
c
d
e
f
g
h
i
j
k
l
m
n
o
p
q
r
s
t

Fig. 70 Embellishment detail: Pattern 25

Key: (a) and **(b)** Row of crewel stitch
(c) Fly-stitched stem
(d) and **(e)** Crewel and chain-stitched branch
(f) Garnet bead fruit
(g) Variegated 4mm silk embroidery ribbon in pierced leaf stitch
(h) Chain-stitched line B
(i) Herringbone-stitched row
(j) Chain-stitched line A
(k) Back-stitched couching
(l) UltraSuede shoulder
(m) Over feather of 4mm silk embroidery ribbon in pierced leaf stitch
(n) Under feather
(o) Inked detail in black Pigma Micron 01 pen
(p) Tail feather of 4mm silk embroidery ribbon in pierced leaf stitch
(q) UltraSuede leg, silk thread edge-embroidered in blanket stitch
(r) 3mm yellow picot-edged trim
(s) and **(t)** Chain-stitched rows

Variations

- *Pattern 24*'s Herringbone wreath is framed on the outside by another row of the chain stitch. Then two facing rows of blanket stitch are worked in antique gold embroidery thread. The final outer frame is 3mm-wide antique gold braid.
- *Pattern 26*'s Herringbone wreath is embroidered in overdyed pearl cotton size 3, then bounded on the outside by a second chain-stitched row of the same. At Line C, two facing rows of blanket stitch are worked in antique gold embroidery thread. The final outer frame is overdyed size 3 pearl cotton couched with antique gold embroidery thread. To the right of the frame a needleful of the pearl cotton has been plopped down (its end pulled by needle to the back) and couched in a relaxed free-form style.
- *Pattern 27*'s outer wreath is formed simply from two rows of purchased trim: a narrow 2mm gold braid trim is framed by a twisted Mokuba cord. The herringbone is stitched with two strands of size 5 pearl cotton and one of antique gold embroidery thread, threaded into the same needle.

"Cameo Portrait: Moment of Wonder" by Elly Sienkiewicz

Pattern 24 "Cameo Portrait: Moment of Wonder"

PROCEDURE/APPLIQUÉ APPROACH

Begin Pattern 24 (page 121) by making its frame as described in Embroidered Wreaths of Fancy Sampler Quilt II (page 63). To appliqué the central figures, follow the procedure on page 52.

EMBELLISHMENT

Tendrils of hair over the maiden's ears begin as UltraSuede appliqué and end drawn in ink. The hot pink cheek is optional. I cut mine using a ¼" self-adhesive office dot as a template. The boughs above the maiden's head are chain stitched in size 5 pearl cotton, then echoed with a row stem stitched in antique gold embroidery thread. The leaves are pierced leaf stitched in hand-dyed 4mm silk embroidery ribbon, the fruits are UltraSuede cut with ¼" self-adhesive office dots. The smaller berry in the dove's mouth is also UltraSuede. Her feathers are pierced leaf stitched 4mm silk embroidery ribbon. Her eye is a tiny French knot in the same antique gold embroidery thread that embellishes her beak,

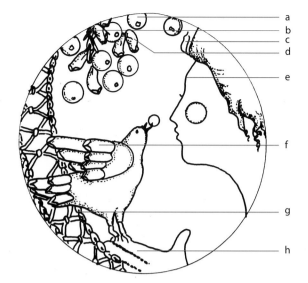

Fig. 71 Embellishment detail, "Moment of Wonder" Pattern 24

Key: (**a**) UltraSuede berry appliqué
(**b**) Crewel and chain stitched branch
(**c**) Pigma Micron pen drawn detail
(**d**) Pierced leaf stitched 4mm silk embroidery ribbon
(**e**) Black Pigma Micron 01 pen drawn outline of figures
(**f**) Pierced leaf stitched 4mm silk ribbon feathers
(**g**) Chain stitched Line A, oval frame
(**h**) Crewel stitch in silk 100 sewing thread to define fingers

legs, and claws, and the fruits' French knots. The girl is outlined in black Pigma Micron 01 pen. Stray locks and eyelashes are penned in.

"Cameo Portrait: Recognition of Intelligence" by Elly Sienkiewicz

"Cameo Portrait: Tender Souls" by Elly Sienkiewicz

Pattern 25
"Cameo Portrait: Recognition of Intelligence"

PROCEDURE/APPLIQUÉ APPROACH/
EMBELLISHMENT

Make Pattern 25's (page 121) frame as described in Embroidered Wreaths of Fancy Sampler Quilt II (page 63). To appliqué the central figures, follow All About UltraSuede Appliqué (page 52). The crow's feathers are variegated 4mm silk ribbon, pierced leaf stitched. His eye is a antique gold embroidery thread French knot. He holds a garnet berry in his mouth. The boy is outlined in black Pigma Micron 01 pen.

Pattern 26
"Cameo Portrait: Tender Souls"

PROCEDURE/APPLIQUÉ APPROACH/
EMBELLISHMENT

Stitch Pattern 26's (page 122) frame as described in Embroidered Wreaths of Fancy Sampler Quilt II (page 63). To appliqué the central figures, follow the steps in All About UltraSuede Appliqué (page 52). The bluebird's base is blue UltraSuede. A layer of 7mm silk ribbon is needleturn appliquéd over its breast, back, and head. Its wing and tail feathers are pierced leaf stitch taken in 4mm silk ribbon. The bird has touches of embroidery—beige silk thread, crewel stitched at the shoulder, antique gold embroidered feet and French knot eye—and an inked beak holding a bead berry. The boy is outlined in black Pigma Micron 01 pen.

"Cameo Portrait: Cherubs" by Elly Sienkiewicz

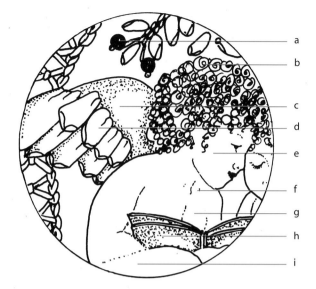

Fig. 72 Embellishment detail, Pattern 27

Key: **(a)** Garnet bead fruit with a seed bead base
(b) French knot curls in mixed threads
(c) UltraSuede wing-shoulder
(d) Pierced leaf stitched feathers in 7mm silk embroidery ribbon
(e) UltraSuede appliqué cheek, padded underneath with thin batting cut to shape
(f) and **(g)** Neck and breastbone stab stitched, sculpted with fine sewing silk
(h) UltraSuede book inserted into a slit in the cherub, appliquéd, then crewel stitch accented in antique gold embroidery thread
(i) Note that the cherub on the left is a different shade of UltraSuede than the cherub on the right

Pattern 27
"Cameo Portrait: Cherubs"

PROCEDURE/APPLIQUÉ APPROACH

Begin Pattern 27 (page 122) by making its frame as described in Embroidered Wreaths (page 63). To appliqué the central figures, follow the steps in All About UltraSuede Appliqué (page 52) with the following exception:

Cut the cherub appliqués out of thin dense batting. Then cut these batting shapes down by ⅛" all around. Gluestick the batting shapes in place over the background cloth. Gluestick the UltraSuede appliqués over the batting shapes. The appliqué is slit above the knee and forearms to allow the book to slip under. The chin-lines are slit open above the chests as a soft-sculpture technique. Slip a bit of extra batting under the heads, chests, knees, and thighs. Catch the chest in appliquéing each chin down. With fine silk thread and a #11 milliners needle, take a few tack stitches (at chin lines, chest, arms, and thighs) to mold the UltraSuede's shape realistically.

EMBELLISHMENT

French knot the cherubs' curls in size 3 pearl cotton, overdyed. On the left-hand angel, four strands of floss are threaded in the same needle as a strand of antique gold embroidery thread for the "dark roots" look. Some over-the-cheek curls begin as embroidery and are completed by inkwork. The wing feathers are layered from the bottom up in two rows of pierced leaf stitch taken in 7mm variegated silk ribbon. The book is outline stitched in antique gold embroidery thread, while garnet bead fruit are attached with a seed bead finale. Finish by penning the body outlines and facial features in black Pigma Micron 005 pen. Colored pencils shade the bodies' roundness (use pink, yellow, and salmon) closest to the sewn edges. Color cheeks and rouge lips.

Independent Study

Set your design talent free by stitching these four wreath challenge recipes, each on a 9" background square:

1. Mark a 5" diameter circle, centered, and appliqué a bias wreath stem to it by Method 2 (page 60). Ornament the wreath with floral appliqués.

2. Mark a double circle (⅛" apart) with a 5" inside diameter. Appliqué a bias wreath stem to it by Method 3 (page 61). Ornament the wreath with fruit appliqués.

3. Pencil Pattern 22's (page 111) heart, centered, on a background square. Embellish the drawn wreath stem with silk ribbon embroidered flowers and bead embroidery. For inspiration, see "Fancywork Heart," pictured at right.

4. Pencil Pattern 22's heart, centered, on a background square. Embellish the drawn wreath stem with wired ribbon flowers and leaves from *Romancing Ribbons into Flowers*. For inspiration, see "Flowering Heart," pictured at right.

"Fancywork Heart" by Carol Warner Mesimer

"Flowering Heart" by Sherry Cook

LESSON 7

Where's the Embroidery in "Broderie Perse?"

*Whatever makes an impression on the heart seems
lovely in the eye.*

Sa'di, "Gulistan" (1258)

Fancywork tours the world, taking on new tools and techniques! Lesson 7 revels in such joyful basics as creative collage, exotic textiles, tempting textures, buttonhole and blanket stitch, *broderie Perse*, and birds. Though splendidly simple, these tools are among fancy appliqué's most inspiring treasures.

Materials

For basic supplies, see Appliqué Supplies, page 12.

PATTERN 28
Appliqué (Layer A) requires scraps backed with fusible bonding web: 4¾" square of Thai silk dupioni, 6" scrap of medium-size floral print; scraps of cotton for hearts and bird.
Background (Layer B) 9" square of cotton solid

PATTERN 29
Appliqué (Layer A): Fusible bonding-backed scraps of cotton for hearts and bird
Background (Layer B): 9" square of cotton print

PATTERN 30
Appliqué (Layer A): 9" square of fusible bonding-backed cotton floral print; scraps of a red cotton solid (fusible backed) for the bird; white Ultra-Suede for eye.
Background (Layer B): 9" square of cotton plaid

Supplies for Embellishment

PATTERN 28
Embroidery floss; 4mm silk embroidery ribbon; antique gold embroidery thread.

PATTERN 29
Buttonhole twist, antique gold embroidery thread; Tire silk thread in red; embroidery floss; 4mm silk embroidery ribbon.

PATTERN 30
Scraps of fusible bonding-backed UltraSuede for beak, eye, body, wings, and tail; size 9 shaded, wired ribbon, fusible-backed for wing's shoulders and back; silk embroidery floss, silk thread, 4mm and 7mm silk embroidery ribbon; black Pigma Micron 01 pen.

Collage and Chintzwork: Two of Fancy Appliqué's Most Festive Options

collage *n.—An artistic composition of materials and objects pasted over a surface. (From the French coller, to glue.)*
Collage injects spontaneity into appliqué and coaxes a realist toward impressionism. Bonding textiles, tints, and textures endows appliqué with a scrap quilt's freedom. Ribbon flowers, bright insects, and appliquéd birds dance in my dreams, but where to stitch them into a quilt? Collage is the perfect solution. It is the boundless backdrop, the entrée for rich

stitchery, the epitome of artful display. Quicker and easier than representational appliqué, collage's abstraction—as witness Victorian "Crazies"—enhances a bright splash of appliquéd realism.

Bonding characterizes collage. Even nineteenth century chintz collage rested on glue, a recipe for which is cited in T. de Dilmont's *Encyclopedia of Needlework*. Contemporary chintzwork (print motifs cut out, heat-bonded to the background, and edge-stitched) uses fusible webs, to ease stitchery. This lesson's three blocks just begin to open a trove of possibilities by mixing unstitched edges, frayed silk, ribbons, threads, print cut-outs, abstract and representational shapes, and plaids mixed with plains. In addition to being a progression of collage techniques, Patterns 28, 29, and 30 begin the evolution of bird appliqué from simple to ever more complex. Though simple, this lesson's blocks promise you an appliqué quilt whose whole is greater than the sum of its parts!

Where's the Embroidery in "Broderie Perse"?

embroider v.—*1. To embellish with needlework.*
2. To add embellishments or fanciful details.

Broderie Perse translates as "Persian Embroidery." In its original usage, *broderie Perse* referred to cut-out print motifs sewn to the background by a decorative off-white stitch in a heavier thread. In the early nineteenth century's most elegant *broderie Perse* quilts, this same off-white thread embellishes details within the print itself. This further embroidery can consist of blanket stitch, buttonhole stitch, crewel stitch, or chain stitch. These stitches may be done over a leaf's veins or edging a flower's petals, making the appliqué ornate, textural, and "encrusted with embroidery." What we moderns have called *broderie Perse* would more appropriately be called chintzwork. In chintzwork, the cut-outs are edge-stitched, but have no interior embroidery. With fusible bonding webs, chintz's tight weave is no longer necessary for edge-stitching, so any appealing cotton print motif now suits this needleart. In the front cover's "Grackles and Grapes" square, I stitched its grape print bower in a contemporary *broderie Perse* style. Please look at the front cover, for that block's stylistic details can be applied to this lesson's patterns as well:

Threads

Rather than in the off-white thread of traditional *broderie Perse*, the grape cut-outs' embroidery is done in threads of different sizes, different fibers (cotton, silk, wool, rayon, metallic), and different colors.

Edge-fused Appliqué

1. Before cutting out the print motif, fuse the bonding web just ¾" deep around the motif's outer edge. (Edge-fusing is taught in *Dimensional Appliqué*, pages 31-32.)

2. Trim the unfused bonding web away from the print motif's center.

3. Cut a tiny margin (¹⁄₃₂") beyond the print motif to allow room for the blanket stitching.

Fancy Appliqué

4. Gluestick thin cotton batting (cut ⅛" smaller all around the perimeter) to the wrong side of a printed grape bunch, padding it. Next, heat-bond the print motif's edges to the background cloth.

5. Quilt the outline of the grapes with large running stitches (to be covered by embroidery).

6. Cut a few accent grapes from vintage or contemporary rayon ribbon, seal the cut edges with clear nail polish, then blanket stitch the grapes onto the print. In the front cover photo, these accents are the brighter grapes and the velvet grapes.

7. Cut purple Mokuba Organdy Ribbon to cover one bunch of grapes, then edge-seal and blanket stitch it to the print. Can you find the organdy overlaid grapes in the photo?

It is the right-hand bunch.

Edge-stitching

I used both the blanket stitch and the tailor's buttonhole stitch to edge-stitch the print. Why not try all of the edge stitches taught on page 39? A comprehensive embroidery book will offer yet more blanket stitch variations. Vary your threads and stitches, and embroider both raw edges and the print's interior—all as you please! Such stitchery's delights are manifold. Years ago, when first I saw a true *broderie Perse* antique quilt, I never imagined that I would ever attempt this needleart. But having reached for the cover block's challenge, I loved every minute of its fancywork.

"Red Bird in the Garden" by Elly Sienkiewicz

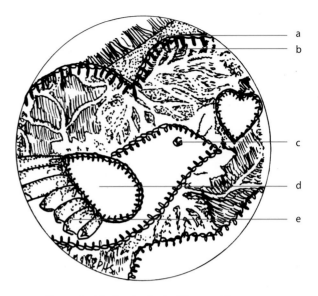

Fig. 73 "Red Bird in the Garden" (Pattern 28)

Key: (a) Collaged appliqué. A pulled-thread fringe, ¹/₄" deep
   (b) Blanket stitch edge-embroidery
   (c) French knot eye in antique gold embroidery thread
   (d) Wing shoulder
   (e) Single layer of wing feathers in 4mm silk, pierced leaf stitched

Pattern 28
"Red Bird in the Garden"

PROCEDURE/APPLIQUÉ/EMBELLISHMENT

For full instructions, see Collage and Chintzwork, pages 69-70.

1. This block's collage backdrop is a 4¾" fancy fabric square, set on point and heat-bonded to Layer B. The Thai silk dupioni pictured has a ¼" deep fringe of pulled threads. Dab clear nail polish to seal the fringe at each corner.

2. Compose the collage of heart shapes (Pattern 28, page 123), floral elements cut from a print, and the red bird. Gluestick-baste the fusible-backed cloth and ribbon shapes, then heat-bond the collage in place.

3. Blanket-stitch the other appliqués' edges, but for emphasis (and for the joy of it) tailor's buttonhole-stitch (page 39) the bird.

4. Embroider a single layer of wing feathers on the bird with pierced leaf stitch in 4mm silk ribbon. Begin the feathers just below the wing-shoulder's buttonhole stitch. Gluestick-baste, then stitch the UltraSuede eye and beak. Note that this bird is the simplest in this lesson's stylistic progression of three bird patterns.

5. Add a bit of silk ribbon embroidery to give the flowers dimension.

6. With embroidery floss, French knot the flower centers and the bird's eye.

7. Where artistic, crewel stitch the leaf veins and buttonhole stitch the flower petals.

"Dove in the Vineyard" by Elly Sienkiewicz

"Red Bird in Paradise" by Elly Sienkiewicz

Pattern 29
"Dove in the Vineyard"

PROCEDURE/APPLIQUÉ/EMBELLISHMENT
For full instructions, see Collage and Chintzwork, pages 69-70.
This wee bird does not really resemble a dove, but it is more realistic than the appliquéd bird of Pattern 28.
1. Begin the collage on a background print. That print should give the block its theme.
2. Heat-bond the dove and hearts composition into place.
3. Edge-stitch the appliqués. Relish the hearts' invitation to varied stitch embellishment!
4. With 4mm silk ribbon, pierced leaf stitch the bottom wing feathers. Begin each stitch at the wing-shoulder and finish at wing tip. Begin a second, shorter row of pierced leaf stitch at the wing-shoulder.
5. Make the bird's eye with a French knot and embroider his beak, both in antique gold embroidery thread.
6. Embroider a unit of the background print in *broderie Perse* style (page 70).

Pattern 30
"Red Bird in Paradise"

PROCEDURE/APPLIQUÉ/EMBELLISHMENT
Pattern 30 has three goals: to include a geometric fabric; to push *broderie Perse* dramatically into the third dimension with silk ribbon; and to appliqué a more realistic bird. Red Bird has six of the anatomical identifiers bird-watchers look for: head, back, beak, breast, wings, and tail. (Lesson 8 completes that list with legs and feet.) The forked tail and characteristic wingspread are those of a Purple Martin, though the color is not. If such things intrigue you, make a bird guide your appliqué companion!
1. Make a contact paper template of Pattern 30's bird (page 123). Cut the body (head, back, beak, breast, wings, and tail) from fusible bonding-backed cotton as a single piece. Add no seam allowance.
2. For Layer B, use a plaid or stripe, perhaps to convey the look of farmed fields?
3. Cut windows in Layer A's floral print, creating a cloud-like pattern to reveal the background. Heat-bond the floral cut-out to Layer B.
4. **Red Bird:** Adjust Red Bird's placement to your floral print, then heat-bond him to Layer A. (Create drama in the bird/print layout. Here, Red Bird has a long view with places to go and things to do.)

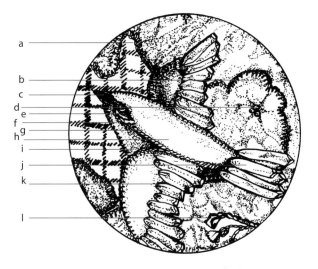

Fig. 74 "Red Bird in Paradise" (Pattern 30)

Key: (**a**) Blanket edge-stitching on the floral cut-out
    (**b**) Interior (not on the raw edge) print embellishment in blanket stitch
    (**c**) Black UltraSuede beak
    (**d**) Floss French knot accent over a print flower
    (**e**) Eye cut from a white UltraSuede swatch, then embellished in ink and thread
    (**f**) Silk thread crewel-stitched detail
    (**g**) Silk thread crewel edge-stitching
    (**h**) The back, appliquéd in heat-bonded shaded wired ribbon
    (**i**) Body, wings, and tail are all UltraSuede appliqués
    (**j**) Tail feathers are 4mm silk, pierced leaf stitched from the outside in, so that the central feather lays on the top
    (**k**) Wing feathers
    (**l**) Silk buttonhole twist and 4mm silk ribbon buds embroidered over the print cut-out

5. Cut the back and wing-shoulder units from fusible-backed shaded wired ribbon, then heat-bond them to the body.

6. Crewel stitch the back's interior edge (g) using 50 weight Tire silk thread in red, doubled.

7. Appliqué the beak in black UltraSuede. Crewel stitch the line between the upper and lower beak in black silk thread.

8. Pierced leaf stitch the wing feathers in 4mm silk ribbon. Begin each stitch about ⅛" inside the fused ribbon shoulder appliqué and finish at wing's tip. Embroider the feathers beginning from the wing tip and progressing in toward the body.

9. Begin the tail feather stitches just within the ribbon back. Finish each pierced leaf stitch just beyond the bonded cotton tail. Pierced leaf stitch on both sides from the outside of the tail to the inside so that the feathers fan out.

10. Blanket stitch all remaining visible edges of the bird appliqué. Use a fine matching sewing thread (cotton machine embroidery thread or silk, 50-60 weight), doubled.

11. Determine eye position, using the pattern and a pin-piercing technique. Mark the eye with a dot. Cut the eye out of white UltraSuede and appliqué it. At the last (to avoid smudging), ink the eye heavily, leaving only its highlight white. Heat set with an iron using a fine press cloth. Crewel stitch the lines under the eye in matching Tire silk sewing thread.

Embellishing the *Broderie Perse* Cut-Out: Blanket stitch the visible raw edges of the botanical cut-out. Accent the floral print with loop-stitched five-petaled flowers (page 31). Use variegated 7mm silk embroidery ribbon and French knot the centers with silk floss. Disperse small embroidered elements (petals, buds, centers, stems, leaf veins) among other printed flowers, mixing embellished and unembellished prints.

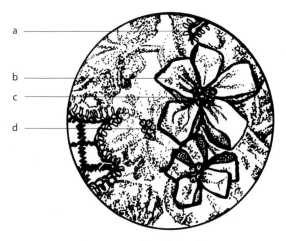

Fig. 75 Looped flower detail, Pattern 30

Key: (**a**) Blanket stitching on the cut-out's edge
    (**b**) 7mm silk looped ribbon flower
    (**c**) Silk floss French knot centers
    (**d**) Embroidered print flower center

LESSON 8

Creature Creations

No ladder needs the bird, but skies
To situate its wings,
Nor any leader's grim baton
Arraigns it as it sings.

—Emily Dickinson (1883)

Defying predictions of a silent spring, backyard birds seem yearly more numerous. Just before dawn, they wake us to song, peopling even urban landscapes with a friendly presence ever willing to bob for a crumb or to carry our thoughts skyward. These miraculous creatures, gifted with flight, are readily tamed into needleworks bright.

Materials

For basic supplies, see Appliqué Supplies, page 12.

PATTERN 31
Appliqué (Layer A): 5" scrap of variegated sky blue, fusible backed; ¾ yard Artemis bias-cut satin or silk, 2" wide; for the Holly Wreath: three 7" cuts in Earthmother; for the Cardinal: 5" cut in Hotflash. Background (Layer B): 9" square of cotton print

PATTERN 32
Appliqué (Layer A): 5" scrap of variegated sky blue, fusible backed; for the Holly Wreath: Artemis bias-cut satin or silk ribbon, 2"-wide; three 7" cuts in Earthmother.
Ribbon A: Artemis bias-cut satin or silk, 1½"-wide x 9" in French Toast
Ribbon B: 1½"-wide x 3" cut of vintage rayon ribbon shaded pinkish to ripe peach
Background (Layer B): 9" square of cotton print

PATTERN 33
Appliqué (Layer A): 5" scrap of variegated sky blue, fusible backed; black UltraSuede 6" swatch for body, 5" swatch of a second shade of black for the wings; 3" scrap of gray for eye, beak, and legs.
Background (Layer B): 9" square of cotton print

Supplies for Embellishment

PATTERN 31
DMC Antique Gold and Antique Silver embroidery thread; rose overdyed size 5 pearl cotton; two shades of white embroidery floss (one in size 5 pearl cotton, one six-strand floss); pine green cotton floss, variegated rayon floss, and Needle Necessities UltraSuede Thread (loden green) or Mokuba Suede Tape (#1509, 2mm, color 16) for evergreen needles; *Branch*: black Mokuba Beaded Yarn (#0140, color 3) or overdyed chenille yarn (from Quilter's Resource, Chicago, #4028, Olive/wine); ¼" x 18" gilt-edged green "lettuce" trim (also from Quilter's Resource); ¼"-wide looped beige trim; 2mm-wide antique gold braided trim; clear seed beads for snow; black seed beads for eyes; variegated red silk embroidery ribbon in 4mm and 7mm; ⁷⁄₁₆"-wide Artemis bias-cut ribbon in Hotflash for wing tips; black Pigma Micron 005 and 01 pens; Pigma Brush pens; colored pencils.

PATTERN 32
Antique gold embroidery thread; 2mm-wide antique gold braided trim; 3mm yellow picot trim; fine gold thread; clear seed beads; garnet bead berries; colored pencils.

PATTERN 33

Antique silver embroidery thread; miniature red silk soutache braid; 4mm-wide antique gold braided trim; miniature yellow picot trim; variegated black silk embroidery ribbon in 4mm and 7mm; black Pigma Micron 005 and 01 pens; 50 weight Tire silk thread in dark gray and in black; charcoal gray colored pencil; seed beads (clear glass and berry colored); *Ribbon leaves*: Cut 21 lengths of ⅝" x 2" French wired ribbon, shaded from light to dark pine green. Stitch as shown in Figure 76. *Bittersweet berries*: Cut ¼" circles of UltraSuede in three shades, from orange to salmon, and about ⅓ as many UltraSuede circles in mustard and loden. Clip ⅔ of the way through these latter circles at their midpoint so that they can be opened up to form the husks of certain of the bittersweet berries (see Figure 80, h).

The Circular Wreaths of Fancy Sampler Quilt II

Fancy Sampler Quilt II (page 11) sports five porthole-centered, botanically-wreathed squares; three are in this lesson. The fourth, the quilt's dove center, is in Lesson 11. The fifth showcases Lesson 12's frog. While their bird-inhabited centers differ, Lesson 7's three blocks share initial similarities of construction.

Prepare Pattern 31

1. Cut out Pattern 31's (page 124) sky blue porthole and heat-bond it, centered, onto Layer B.
2. Trace Pattern 31's porthole and holly wreath frame, centered, onto a 9" scrap of fusible bonding web. Cut out the porthole portion to avoid double bonding.
3. Iron the pattern-marked fusible web, centered, to the wrong side of Layer B. Avoid ironing the excess web (1" beyond the holly leaf wreath) then trim it off.
4. Cut out Layer B's holly leaves on the traced line. Remove the protective paper.
5. Put gluestick (for basting) on the fusible web around the holly cut-outs. Finger-press the three 2" x 7" silk/satin ribbon cuts (right side ribbon to web side cloth) to cover all the holly leaf cut-outs.
6. With a Teflon® press cloth over the ribbon, heat-bond the ribbon to the background.

7. Trace Pattern 31's interior appliqués onto contact paper, then cut out. Drawing around the bird and branch templates, mark their placement on the sky blue circle.

Construct Pattern 31's Holly Wreath Frame

1. Baste the lettuce trim (Figure 77, page 77) so that its gold ruffle faces inward and its flat edge lays on top of the porthole's raw edge.
2. Baste a ¼" looped beige trim (k) so that the loops hide all but the ⅛" ruffle of the lettuce trim. Seal the beginning and end of both trims with clear nail polish, abutting them under the cover of the cardinal's tail feathers, which you will add later. Tack stitch the inner and outer rim of the looped trim.
3. Add color with a row of chain stitch (o) taken over the looped trim. Overdyed size 5 pearl cotton, doubled, was used in the original.
4. Baste, then stitch the antique gold braided trim (f) in place. Seal the cut ends and overlap by ½". Sew one on top of the other as tightly and unobtrusively as possible.
5. Crewel stitch the swag (e) in antique gold embroidery thread.
6. Again in antique gold, crewel stitch (c) each holly leaf's raw edge. Catch a ¹⁄₁₆" bite of the background with each stitch. Running stitch each leaf's center vein (d) in the same gold thread.
7. Berries emerge from the lower right of each leaf. Stitch clusters of beads and 4mm silk ribbon French knots. The snow drifts leftward and is worked in two shades of white (size 5 pearl cotton and six strands of cotton floss) with the occasional crystalline sparkle of a clear seed bead.

Prepare Pattern 32's Holly Wreath

Pattern 32's (page 124) wreath is prepared much the same as Pattern 31's with the following two exceptions:

1. Outline the blue center with yellow picot trim (Figure 78, i). Embroider a seed bead over each picot (j).
2. Stitch three garnet berries (h) to the right of each holly leaf.
3. Trace the fledgling and swirls to the blue center.
4. Embroider the swirls (g) with antique gold embroidery thread in the caught thread stitch.

Prepare Pattern 33's Bittersweet Wreath

1. Heat-bond Pattern 33's (page 125) blue circle, centered, to a 9" background square.
2. Trace Pattern 33's bird, swirls, and leaf placement lines onto the blue cloth porthole.
3. **Boat leaves** (Figure 76): Fold a ⅝" x 2" shaded wired ribbon in half, wired edge on top of wired edge. Leaving a ¼" seam allowance at each raw edged end, running stitch a boat shape, as shown, through both layers. Pull the thread to gather the leaf down to 1⅛" long. Tuck the upper corners under at Folds 2 and 3, then open the boat-stitched ribbon into an oval boat-shaped leaf.

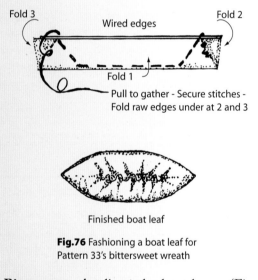

Fold 3   Fold 2
Wired edges
Fold 1
Pull to gather - Secure stitches -
Fold raw edges under at 2 and 3

Finished boat leaf

Fig.76 Fashioning a boat leaf for Pattern 33's bittersweet wreath

4. **Bittersweet**: Appliqué the boat leaves (Figure 5, g) onto the wreath by tack or stab stitch.
5. Using ¼" self-adhesive office dots as templates, cut a handful of UltraSuede bittersweet berries and, arranging by eye, tack them to the wreath, accenting each with a French knot of antique silver embroidery thread. Cut two-thirds of the way through the ¼" husk circles (h). Open each and appliqué it over an UltraSuede circle to reveal a berry-red wedge.
6. **Free-form embroidery ("Plopped Thread")**: Bring a #26 chenille needle threaded with antique silver up from under the block (k) and let the thread drop gracefully into a puddle. Put the needle back through an inch or two from where you came up and couch (using a second milliners needle and black Nymo thread) every ⅜". String clear glass seed beads and black berry

seed beads in batches of three, five, or seven at a time to bead-embroider over the silver thread. When five or more beads are strung, the bead-string must itself be couched. With a U-turn (the bead-carrying needle brought up and reinserted at almost the same point), a couched strand of five beads looks like a berry bunch.

7. **Caught stitch swirl embroidery**: Stitch the swirls in antique silver embroidery thread, catching a blue background cloth thread every 1/16" or so. You'll soon find you can do these by eye, without pre-marking.

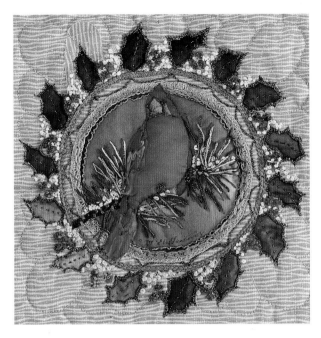

"Cardinal in the Snow" by Elly Sienkiewicz

Pattern 31
"Cardinal in the Snow"

PROCEDURE/APPLIQUÉ/EMBELLISHMENT

For full instructions, see The Circular Wreaths (page 75). The cardinal teaches the basics of raised and embroidered appliqué, a relative to that ancient needleart called Stumpwork. Lesson 12 touches on Stumpwork's history and its sculptural potential.

1. Make three contact paper templates for the cardinal (Pattern 31, page 124): the head/body/right wing unit, the left wing, and the tail. Trace the neck and right wing lines on the body template and slit the lines partially, stencil style. Before removing the contact paper's protective backing, draw the cardinal appliqué (and the branch placement) on a sky blue circle.

2. Cut the tail and left wing/foot unit out of red UltraSuede. Glue-baste these to the blue background.

3. Cut the head/body/right wing (the body unit) a full ¹⁄₁₆" bigger all around than the template. Finger-press the body template to the wrong side of red UltraSuede.

4. Cut thin batting ⅛" smaller all around than the body unit template. Glue this batting within the background's drawn body shape on the blue background.

Fig. 77 "Cardinal in the Snow", embellishment detail

Key: (**a**) Holly berries in 4mm red silk embroidery ribbon and seed beads
(**b**) French knot snow in cotton and seed beads
(**c**) Crewel stitch in antique gold embroidery thread
(**d**) Running stitch
(**e**) Crewel stitch in antique gold embroidery thread
(**f**) Antique gold braided trim
(**g**) Beige UltraSuede beak/cheek appliqué
(**h**) Black seed bead eye
(**i**) Black Pigma Micron 01 pen embellished details
(**j**) Pigma Brush pen and colored pencil highlights
(**k**) Looped trim
(**l**) Pigma Micron pen stippling
(**m**) Padded breast
(**n**) Red UltraSuede wing-shoulder
(**o**) Pearl cotton chain stitching
(**p**) Gilt-edged green lettuce trim
(**q**) Top feather layer (stitched fourth) in 7mm silk, pierced leaf stitched
(**r**) Straight-stitched pine needles in rayon and cotton floss and antique gold embroidery thread
(**s**) Feather layer (stitched third) in 4mm silk embroidery ribbon
(**t**) Bottom feather layer (stitched second) in 4mm silk embroidery ribbon
(**u**) French knot snow
(**v**) Wing tips (stitched first)

5. Glue-baste the UltraSuede body unit over the batting. Baste through the three layers in a triangle (three big stitches) at the body center.

6. Line the UltraSuede edges up with the background markings and appliqué the body. Then appliqué the left wing, but not the tail. (The body's ¹⁄₁₆" easement allows the padded UltraSuede to be appliquéd without distorting the background.)

7. Cut a second body unit out of red bias-cut satin ribbon, this time adding a full ½" seam. Seal the cut edges with clear nail polish.

8. Cut a pointed egg-shaped layer of batting (to include the face). Cut this shape ¼" smaller than the finished UltraSuede head/breast unit. Glue-stick this batting in place over the appliquéd UltraSuede base to round out the breast and face.

9. Position the satin body appliqué over this club sandwich of UltraSuede, batting, and background.

10. With silk thread, big-stitch baste all layers from the base of the body up into the head.

11. Finely appliqué the satin to the drawn outline of the bird, beginning on the right side. Much of its generous seam allowance will be tucked under. Pierce each appliqué stitch into the drawn seamline to contain and shape all the layers. Take only moderately spaced stitches when you sew from the bird's right shoulder to the base of the body, for this wing will be covered by embroidered feathers.

12. **Appliqué the bird's UltraSuede left wing** and needleturn under the satin breast above it, leaving the UltraSuede wing itself, uncovered.

13. In pierced leaf stitch, embroider the tail (one layer) and wing (two layers) of under-feathers in 4mm silk ribbon. The wing tips are stitched with a ⁷⁄₁₆" Artemis bias-cut ribbon threaded on a #22 chenille needle. With the same stitch, embroider the tail and wing's top layer in 7mm silk ribbon.

14. Embroider the bird's feet in antique gold embroidery thread.

15. **Couch the pine bough:** While I used black Mokuba Beaded Yarn for the branch, overdyed pearl cotton or chenille would also work. The pine needles are straight stitches taken with antique gold metallic thread and three strands of colored floss all threaded in the same needle. Other long stitches are taken in green Ultra-Suede thread. Seed beads sprinkled among white French knots deck the branch with snow.

16. **The bird's face:** Pin-pierce the pattern to mark the eyes and beak corners. Appliqué the beak in beige UltraSuede. Stitch a jet bead for each eye. With a Pigma Brush pen, shade the beak in gold, rounding it out with a rosy colored pencil. Sharpen the beak's shape with a black Pigma Micron 005 pen. Ink the cardinal's classic darkness around beak and eyes. Leaving the inking until the last allows the Pigma to dry (heat set) completely lest it be smudged by further handling.

"Fledgling" by Elly Sienkiewicz

Pattern 32 "Fledgling"

For full instructions, see The Circular Wreaths, page 75. Being a babe of the imagination, even the fledgling's pierced leaf stitched wings are impressionistic. A pierced leaf stitched tuft at its forehead gives a grouse-like look. Its eye is a French knot in antique gold embroidery thread with several wraps around the needle. Its beak is satin stitched, its legs and feet blanket stitched (one side only), all in antique gold. The curlicues of antique gold embroidery thread are in caught stitch (page 76). Fine gold thread echo-quilting reduces the pucker caused by the fledgling's plumpness. Aquarelle colored pencils in brown, peach, and rose softly shade birdie's breast, tummy, and legs.

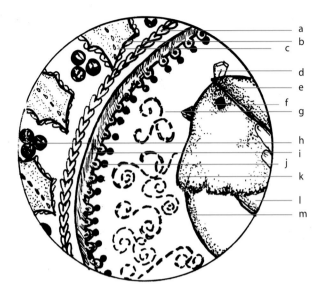

Fig. 78 "Fledgling" embellishment detail

Key: **(a)** Antique gold braid
   (b) Crewel stitch edge appliqué in antique gold embroidery thread
   (c) Gold thread top stitching by running stitch
   (d) Crest, pierced leaf stitched in 4mm silk embroidery ribbon
   (e) Artemis bias-cut, edge-burned silk overlay in French Toast
   (f) French knot eye in antique gold embroidery thread
   (g) Caught-thread swirls in antique gold embroidery thread
   (h) Garnet bead berry
   (i) 1/4" deep yellow picot-edged trim
   (j) Seed bead finial stitched through each picot
   (k) Vintage rayon ribbon overlay appliqué, edge-burned for effect
   (l) Vintage rayon ribbon appliqué with selvage exposed to maximize color contrast
   (m) UltraSuede body appliqué, firmly padded and edge-shaded with colored pencil

1. Stitch Pattern 32's (page 124) wreath, taught on page 75.
2. Make a contact paper template for Pattern 32's fledgling. Trace the fledgling's silhouette onto the blue circle. Trim off the pierced leaf stitched crest (Figure 78, d) and the fluffy breast beyond the dotted line.
3. Cut the legs off the paper template and use them to cut a pair of UltraSuede legs, adding 1/4" above the thigh to layer under the body's appliqué. Tack stitch the UltraSuede legs to the pattern-marked blue circle.
4. Cut a beige UltraSuede body 1/16" bigger all around than the contact paper template. Glue-stick-baste it over three graduated (and glue-basted) batting layers. Make the bottom batting

layer about 1/16" smaller than the seam outline, the middle one 1/4" smaller, and the top one 1/2" smaller.
5. Cut Pattern 32's template into separate A and B ribbon overlay templates. Cut the back and tail overlays from bias-cut Ribbon A with up to 1/2" seam allowance on the upper side only (the lower side—a dotted line on the pattern—does not get seamed under).
6. Cut the breast and wing overlays from Ribbon B, adding the generous 1/2" seam allowance only at the upper, hemmed-under edge. Place the breast template carefully so that the darkest part of the ribbon forms the face and breast as in Pattern 32's photo. On the unhemmed edge, cut a 3/8" allowance beyond the template. Edge-burn that breast edge, passing it through a standing candle's flame. Leaving the template on helps hold the ribbon steady, but take care not to burn your fingers! With a wiped brush of clear nail polish, seal all the ribbon edges including the burnt one. Place the wing area template so that the ribbon's selvage forms the lower side. Layer, then baste the ribbons over the UltraSuede body.
7. Appliqué the ribbons, hemming the upper edges under by needleturn and tack stitching them down. Almost invisibly, stab stitch each ribbon's unhemmed edge with silk 100 thread to hold it in place.
8. Beginning at the tail and moving toward the back, appliqué the outside ribbon edges underneath the UltraSuede, piercing each stitch into the outline drawn on the blue to contain and shape all layers.

"Corvid, the Curious Crow" by Elly Sienkiewicz

Pattern 33
"Corvid, the Curious Crow"

PROCEDURE/APPLIQUÉ/EMBELLISHMENT

For full instructions, see The Circular Wreaths, page 75.
The large Corvid bird family (crows, ravens, and other jet-black beauties) fascinates! Corvid (Pattern 33, page 125), my favorite square in Fancy Sampler Quilt II, is also this lesson's most easily replicated block. Fashion its bittersweet wreath (page 75), then:

Fig.79 Embellishment detail for "Corvid, the Curious Crow"

Key: **(a)** Upper/lower beak division line: quilted, then crewel stitched, both in fine silk thread
(b) UltraSuede beak shaded in colored pencil and pen
(c) Eye edge-embroidered in fine silk thread crewel stitch, then given a French knot at the center and ink embellished
(d) Black Pigma Micron inkwork depicts the crow's unruly neck feathers
(e) The body's UltraSuede shades of black contrasts with that of the wing overlays
(f) Outer wing edge-stitched to drawn outline
(g) Inner wing edge left unsewn
(h) Both wings are cut of the same black UltraSuede shade
(i) The top feathers are the last wing layer to be silk ribbon embroidered

1. Make a contact paper bird template from Pattern 33 (page 125). Trace the crow's silhouette onto the blue circle. Cut the legs off the template and set aside.

2. Cut a padded armature (a sculptor's framework) for the body. Glue-baste very thin compact batting (three graduated layers) to its outline as in Step 4, Pattern 32.

3. Cut the whole bird out of black UltraSuede, adding a ¹⁄₁₆" padding easement allowance beyond the template.

4. Next cut the template into its parts. Place these smaller appliqué templates to UltraSuede's right-side up and cut, adding no seam allowance. (Leave the paper on. It will help the appliqué.) Cut two wings of a second black UltraSuede. Cut the eye, beak, and legs from

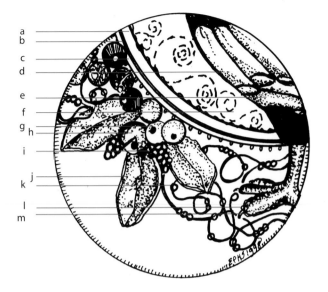

a
b
c
d
e
f
g h
i
k j
l
m

Fig. 80 "Corvid, the Curious Crow" embellishment detail

Key: **(a)** Antique gold braided trim
(b) Red soutache braid
(c) Yellow picot trim
(d) Variegated silk ribbon conveys the luminous quality of feathers. Threading two different shades of black (a 4mm over a 7mm width) is another route to vivacious wing color
(e) The lower layer of feathers is embroidered first
(f) Antique silver embroidery thread worked in caught-thread scrolls
(g) Bittersweet berry of UltraSuede punctuated by an antique silver French knot
(h) Husk is a ¼" UltraSuede circle, slit and appliquéd open, over the berry
(i) Multiple seed beads threaded on the needle, then couch stitched, quickly form clusters
(j) Bittersweet ribbon boat leaves
(k) "Plopped Thread" embroidery, bead-couched
(l) Front leg edges are blanket-stitched in silk sewing thread
(m) Crewel-stitched silk thread edges the back of the leg and underside of the feet

gray. Save the window template (the template from which you cut the eye) to mark the eye's placement.

5. From the paper templates down into Layer B, basting all layers for beak, eye, wings, body, and legs, gluestick, then thread-baste firmly in place. The basting must hold the parts (beak, shoulders, legs) in place while the appliqué stitches force conformance to the drawn outline. If you prefer, baste, then appliqué one unit at a time.

6. Appliqué the outside-wing edges only (Figure 79, f). Tack the inside-wing edges to each other a third of the way down from the shoulder, but leave the edge free (g) above and below that point. The eye, legs, and beak need to be finely tack stitched all around. Stab-stitch quilt, then in sewing thread, crewel stitch the line that divides the upper from the lower beak.

7. Pierced leaf stitch (7mm silk) the single layer of tail feathers. Similarly, fashion the three wing feather layers in 4mm silk ribbon, from the outside to the inside (Figure 80, d), and from the bottom up.

8. Blanket stitch the legs and feet in 50 weight Tire silk thread in dark gray (l). Crewel stitch the back edges of the legs in 50 weight Tire silk thread in black. A black chain stitch forms the claws.

9. Shade the beak with a charcoal gray colored pencil (Figure 79, b). Make a tight French knot pupil (c) in antique silver embroidery thread, or perhaps you have the perfect seed bead for this.

10. Last, use a black Pigma Micron 01 or 005 pen to outline the beak, the eye, and the legs' crinkly skin. Stipple with the pen, sprinkling fine dots (as is in the drawing) to suggest dimension. Heat-set the ink.

He clasps the crag with crooked hands;
Close to the sun in lonely lands,
Ringed with the azure world, he stands.
The wrinkled sea beneath him crawls;
He watches from his mountain walls,
And like a thunderbolt he falls.

—Lord Tennyson, "The Eagle" (1851)

LESSON 9

Ribbon Appliqué~ Flowered & Feathered

*Fair daffodils, we weep to see
You haste away so soon.*

—Robert Herrick (1591-1674) "To Daffodils"

From delicate daffodils to a satin dove on wing, ribbon fancifies this lesson! Domestic, imported, shaded, luminescent, hand-dyed, or vintage, these decorative bands of cloth add romance to our needlework. As a well-tied bow presents the gift, so ribbon, appliquéd, proclaims a needleart's intent.

Materials

For basic supplies, see Appliqué Supplies, page 12.

PATTERN 34
Appliqué (Layer A): 7" scrap of cotton cloth
Background (Layer B): 9" square of cotton cloth

PATTERN 35
Appliqué (Layer A): 9" square of variegated sky blue cotton cloth
Dove appliqué: Quarter yards of 2"-wide Artemis bias-cut satin ribbon in Old Ivory
Background (Layer B): 9" square of off-white printed cotton cloth

Supplies for Embellishment

PATTERN 34
The four daffodils use 46" of size 5 (1" wide or ⅞" wide) of French shaded wired ribbon in yellow. For each of four daffodil *cupped centers*, cut 1" x 3½" length. For each of four daffodil *petal wreaths* , cut 1" x 8" length. Seal raw edges with clear nail polish. The *daffodil leaves* are pierced leaf stitch embroidered from a 13mm-wide variegated silk embroidery ribbon (or rayon knitting ribbon); silk 100 thread; 4mm green silk embroidery ribbon for stems.

PATTERN 35
Dove: 4mm and 7mm silk embroidery ribbon in variegated white for feathers, and a scrap of brown UltraSuede for beak; black Pigma Micron 01 pen; colored pencils. *Flowers*: 7mm variegated silk embroidery ribbon in hydrangea colors; ⅝"-wide Artemis bias-cut silk in Lavender Rose Bud; yellow 4mm silk embroidery ribbon for French knot centers. *Smaller leaves*: ½"-wide Mokuba Luminous Ribbon (#4599, color 7); 7mm green silk embroidery ribbon. *Two large leaves*: green ¾" vintage rayon ribbon. *Letter*: scraps of 1½"-wide Artemis bias-cut silk in Moon Goddess for envelope, in Valentina for heart; variegated blue 4mm silk embroidery ribbon for the letter's tie; set of Pigma Brush pens.
The metallic bow: ⅜" x 12" strip of Lion's Firefly metallic wire-edged ribbon in Blush. (Cut the ribbon ends in a swallow-tail "V." Fringe them softly by fussing at the raw edge with your fingers, then seal the edge with clear nail polish.)

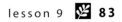

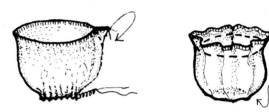

Fig.81 Kathy Galos's Ruched Daffodils

"Daffodil Heart" by Kathy Galos

To form daffodil's cup:

1. Tightly U-turn gather the 1" x 3¹/₂" ribbon, pulling the ribbon back to expose both ends of the bottom edge's wires. Twist the two wires together to hold the gathers. Fold the two top wired edges down, making a 45° angle corner. This hides the raw edges and holds the cup together until it is appliquéd.

2. Turn the cup's "seam" to the back. Push the bottom of the cup forward to hide the gathered selvage. Running stitch a line ³/₁₆" parallel to the cup's upper lip. Pull the thread to gather, then secure the thread.

Pattern 34 "Daffodil Heart"

PROCEDURE APPLIQUÉ/EMBELLISHMENT

For complete instructions, see Adept Needleturn Appliqué, pages 14-22.

Dancing a jig of Springs beyond recall, these daffodils cast sunshine on the soul. Kathy entered this block in the Appliqué Academy's 1998 Scholarship Challenge. All about it seems perfect: proportion, color, contrast, and gesture. Three daffodils look uncharacteristically upward, while the fourth, seemingly in the shadows, quietly looks the other way.

1. Make a contact paper template from Pattern 34's (page 125) heart wreath. Paper on top and with a ¼" seam added, needleturn the heart appliqué to the background square.

2. With a chenille needle #22 and 13 mm variegated silk (or rayon) ribbon, pierced leaf stitch five leaves by eye. With a #11 milliners needle and silk 100 thread, stab stitch just inside the leaf edges to hold them to the background.

3. Assemble four daffodils, setting a cup over a wreath (Figure 81). Pin the flowers to the background.

4. Tack or stab stitch each cup to its petal wreath. Hide the raw ribbon edges behind each flower.

5. Pencil in the stems lightly by eye. With 4mm green silk embroidery ribbon, crewel stitch each daffodil's stem.

To form the daffodil's petal wreath:

3. Beginning and ending with a ¹/₄" seam allowance, mark five petals (each 1¹/₂" apart) across the top of the 1" x 8" ribbon. This top edge will lay under the cup. Running stitch in a mountain/valley pattern from right to left.

4. Pull the thread to gather so that each petal thus formed is the size of your thumbprint. Press the curved lower edge petals inward to form points. Pull the ruched ribbon into a wreath, sewing the finishing end to the starting end.

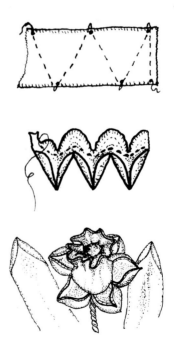

"Messenger of Love" by Elly Sienkiewicz

Pattern 35 "Messenger of Love"

PROCEDURE/APPLIQUÉ APPROACH

A Victorian postcard inspired this block. When that design idea, the perfect ribbons, and my intrigue with mixed media, goldwork, and stumpwork intersected, this block came to life. To begin:

1. Trace Pattern 35's (page 126) circle, bird, and envelope separately onto contact paper then cut these templates out.
2. Pin together two 9" squares, a background square (Layer B) over a sky blue square (Layer A), both right-side up. Trace the circle template onto Layer B and reverse appliqué it to Layer A. (See Reverse Cutaway Appliqué, page 16.) Trim the blue back to 3⁄16" beyond the seam.
3. Trace bird, metallic ribbon's shape, and envelope onto the block for appliqué placement.
4. Appliqué the envelope (as one piece) and then the heart to the block. Quilt a flap outline onto the envelope.
5. Running stitch appliqué the metallic ribbon (just inside selvages) to the block.
6. *The dove*: Cut and label four more bird template units: (A) back, (B) wing-shoulders, (C) head, and (D) the beak.
7. *Back*: Layer three pieces of thin cotton batting, smaller to larger, and gluestick-baste together over Template A's blue cloth outline. The largest

should be just 1⁄8" smaller all around than Template A.

8. Finger-press self-stick Template A to the right side of white satin ribbon. Cut 1⁄2" all around and seal the edge with clear nail polish. Leaving the template on, appliqué both sides of the back, leaving the neck and tail seams open. Running stitch their open seamlines down to Layer B.
9. *Shoulders*: Make two graduated batting layers for each shoulder and proceed as for the back. Baste the wing shoulders in place and appliqué each all around.
10. *Head*: Cut slits in the head template to mark the cheek and eye lines. Follow the same procedure for the head as for the back, again cutting three graduated batting layers. This time stack the layers with the biggest one glue-sticked down first, then the middle one, then the smallest one. (This makes a smoother surface under the silk.) Appliqué the head, leaving the paper on. (The precision of the paper templates should help bring all the bird parts together like a jigsaw puzzle.)
11. *Beak*: Lightly press the beak template (D) to the right side of the UltraSuede. Leave it on and appliqué the beak down with fine tack stitches.

EMBELLISHMENT

12. *Quilting*: Quilt around the crown of the head (p) and the raised center of the back (l), top stitching through to the blue cloth.
13. *Silk ribbon embroidery*: Pierced leaf stitch the tail (two layers in 7mm) and the wings (7mm for the bottom two layers, 4mm for the top). Stitch from the outside in, so that the feathers overlap realistically. Pierced leaf stitch the foliage in 1⁄2"-wide Mokuba Luminous Ribbon and the hydrangeas in variegated 7mm silk embroidery ribbon with French knot centers. The larger hydrangea petals are done with two leaf stitches each, pierced off-center. The largest hydrangea, left of the letter, has 3⁄4"-wide vintage rayon ribbon leaves brought through the fabric by a large needle, looped, folded crisply into a prairie point, then reinserted by needle into the fabric 3⁄16" beyond where it emerged. The letter's ribbon is split stem stitch embroidered (page 116) in 4mm silk ribbon, then shaded with a Pigma Brush pen. The ribbon placement can be penciled onto the block before embroidering.

a
b
c
d
e
f
g
h
i
j
k
l
m
n
o
p
q
r
s
t
u
v

Fig. 82 "Messenger of Love" embellishment details

14. *Ink and Colored Pencil:* Ink the eyes and beak. Add a white gleam with colored pencil. Use the side of a good quality, colored pencil (Aquarelle or Prismacolor in blue, white, and yellow) to shade a cloud pattern in the sky. Scratch the shading with your fingernail to soften the color. To add dimension, shade the bottom edge of the bird's wings and body with just a touch of colored pencil and pen.

Key: (**a**) Pierced leaf stitched 7mm ribbon leaf
(**b**) Wire edged gold mesh ribbon
(**c**) Pierced leaf stitched hydrangea petal
(**d**) yellow 4mm silk ribbon French knot
(**e**) Bottom wing feather layer of 7mm silk ribbon pierced leaf stitched
(**f**) Top wing feather layer
(**g**) Bottom tail feather layer of 7mm silk ribbon pierced leaf stitched
(**h**) Layer A shaded with colored pencil

(**i**) Shoulder appliqué edge: both top and bottom wing feathers begin here
(**j**) Top tail feather layer
(**k**) Pierced leaf stitched leaf. The needle has been reinserted through the ribbon at its right edge so that the leaf's point pulls to the left
(**l**) This layer of the back has been padded and appliquéd over the full body appliqué
(**m**) Shoulder appliqué over graded batting
(**n**) The body contour shadows are augmented by colored pencil shading
(**o**) Silk envelope edge-shaded with ink stippling
(**p**) Crown of the head is separately padded and appliquéd
(**q**) Black Pigma Micron pen drawn eyes and stippled shading
(**r**) UltraSuede beak, ink embellished
(**s**) Red silk heart appliqué
(**t**) Split stem stitched 4mm silk embroidery ribbon
(**u**) Green vintage ribbon, 3/4" wide, stitched (in and out of adjacent holes) and folded into a point
(**v**) Off-center pierced leaf stitched hydrangea petal. For this larger blossom two off-center stitches of 7mm ribbon form one center-pointed petal

LESSON 10

The Heart Wreath Review

From fairest creatures we desire increase,
That thereby beauty's rose might never die.

—W. Shakespeare, *Sonnets* (1609)

Enjoy a challenge? Consider Lesson 10 to be a Comprehensive Exam reviewing lessons learned. Upon completion, award yourself an honorary Master of Arts in Appliqué! Or simply savor wreathing four elegant but differently made rose appliqués. Like a *cabochon*—a precious stone cut in a concave shape—each of these heart-framed blocks will perform, jewel-like, in your Fancywork Album.

Materials

For basic supplies, see Appliqué Supplies, page 12.

PATTERNS 36, 37, 38, AND 39
Appliqué (Layer A): 8" piece of variegated sky blue fabric, fusible-backed
Background (Layer B): 9" square of off-white printed cotton
For the cabochon frames: 3mm-wide antique gold braid trim; ¼"-wide yellow picot trim; overdyed chenille yarn (Quilters Resource, #4028, olive/wine); antique gold embroidery thread.
For rose foliage: 10" scrap of green calico; 3" scraps green UltraSuede (in two shades), 13mm-wide silk embroidery ribbon.
For inscriptions: black Pigma Micron 01 pen

PATTERNS 36, 37, 38, AND 39
For each rosebud: A ⅝" x 3½" length of shaded French wired ribbon; *For each rose:* ⅝" x 15" length of shaded French wired ribbon; **Pattern 36**: Green Pigma Brush pen; black Pigma Micron 01 pen.

Pattern 37: Antique gold embroidery thread; black Nymo thread; green embroidery floss; green sewing thread; clear seed bead; black Pigma Micron 01 and 005 pens. **Pattern 38**: Silk 100 thread; green silk buttonhole twist; green sewing thread; gold metallic thread; yellow Pigma Brush pen; black Pigma Micron 01 pen; *Rosebud*: A ⅞" x 2½" length of shaded French wired ribbon; *Rose*: A ⅞" x 7" length of shaded French wired ribbon. **Pattern 39**: Two 15mm x 1⅛" lengths of Mokuba Velvet Ribbon #4586 in color 7 (from MKB/Mokuba, NYC, see Sources, page 140); two ⅝" x 1½" lengths of vintage striped rayon ribbon, raw edges sealed with clear nail polish; black Pigma Micron 01 pen.

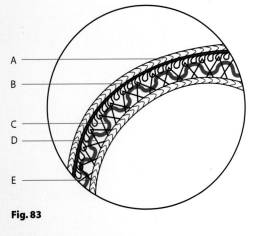

Fig. 83

Key: Trimming the *Cabochon* Frame
Row A—Reproduction antique gold braid—3mm wide
Row B—Reproduction yellow picot trim—4mm wide
Row C—Overdyed rayon chenille yarn
Row D—(Stitched between rows B and E, over C)—
antique gold embroidery thread
Row E—Reproduction 3mm antique gold braid

The *Cabochon* Wreaths of Fancy Album II

Patterns 36 to 39 differ only in inscription and the technique employed to accomplish the rose appliqué. Each frame is glue-basted, then stitched, so they invite assembly-line production. By the time the fourth pattern's frame is laid out, the glue on the first has dried and the trim is ready to appliqué to Layer B. Repeat the following steps for each of the four squares:

1. To guide pattern placement, crease a 9" background square (Layer B) diagonally in half and again into quarters diagonally.
2. Make a full contact paper template for Pattern 36's frame by tracing it over a light box and cutting it double on the fold.
3. Trace the frame and Pattern 36's frame-and-rose appliqué outline onto Layer B.
4. Prepare the blue heart center as described under The Copperplate Inscribed Hearts (page 88).
5. Heat-bond the blue heart center into the frame drawn on the background.
6. As you construct the frame, seal the starting and finishing end of each trim with clear nail polish.
7. With a toothpick, dab white glue along the background of Row A, half a heart at a time. Starting under a leaf (a) glue-baste the antique gold braid trim to the background, folding a "V" to turn the point (b).
8. Abut the braid's finishing end to its starting end at (a).
9. Repeat Steps 6 and 7 for Rows B, C, and E, one at a time and with these differences:
   The heart's trefoil: Tack stitch Row E around each . loop (c), inside edge first. With #11 milliners needle and silk thread, gather the loop's inside curve one-third at a time then tack stitch it down. On the right side of the heart, leave ½" of Row E open so that the rose stem can be tucked under it in due course.
   Row C's chenille: Drop the chenille in airy loops, pressing it lightly onto the glue dots.
10. Row D, the couched herringbone stitch, holds the chenille in place. With a #26 chenille needleful of antique gold embroidery thread, work the herringbone embroidery (page 63) from left to right above the leaf (a), finishing where you began. While the Cameo Portraits of Lesson 6 have herringbone frames bounded by chain stitch, this herringbone is worked between trim Rows B and E, and then couched across the center of each "X."

The Copperplate Inscribed Hearts

The Copperplate (or Spencerian) Hand is a finishing touch on many nineteenth century quilts. This vintage writing can be transferred by iron-on photocopy (page 36) then gone over in ink. It can also be traced over a light box onto a stiffened block (spray starched from the wrong side). Because the trim and rose appliqués interrupt some words, freehand writing, taught below, seems the easiest alternative.

The Prayer of Saint Francis

PATTERN 36 INSCRIPTION

Lord, make me an instrument of thy peace.
Where there is hatred, let me sow love,
Where there is injury, pardon;
Where there is doubt, faith.

—Prayer of Saint Francis, lines 1—4

PATTERN 37 INSCRIPTION

Where there is despair, hope,
Where there is darkness, light;
Where there is sadness, joy.

—Prayer of Saint Francis, lines 5—7

PATTERN 38 INSCRIPTION

Divine Master, grant that I may not
so much seek
To be consoled as to console
To be understood, as to understand
To be loved, as to love.

—Prayer of Saint Francis, lines 8—11

PATTERN 39 INSCRIPTION

For it is in giving that we receive.
It is in pardoning that we are pardoned,
It is in dying to self that we are born to
eternal life.

—Prayer of Saint Francis, lines 12—14

TO INSCRIBE THE HEART FREEHAND

1. Cut the Pattern 36 heart from fusible-backed variegated blue cloth. Remove the fusible's protective paper. The fusible web itself will stabilize the cloth during inscription.
2. On a light box, trace the trefoil outline at heart's top, the rose at its bottom.
3. As a guide only, pin a draft of Pattern 36's inscription centered in place, right side to the block's wrong side.
4. Use a fresh black Pigma Micron 01 pen. The Copperplate Alphabet below may help you inscribe the block. If, as a child, you were taught a slanted script like "Palmer," simply make your writing a bit taller (upper case = 3 x lower case) and thicken each downstroke.

If you care to practice first, write your own name in the Copperplate Hand, then practice capital letters. Ability will follow intent! Use masking tape as a guideline. Do a rough draft on the tape first, then use it as a straight edge on the cloth, writing above it. Lift the tape up, complete letter tails that fall below the line and repeat this process, line by line.

A B C D E F G H I
J K L M N O P Q R
S T U V W X Y Z
abcdefghijklmnopqrsstuvwxyz

The Copperplate Alphabet Roundhand Alphabet by Horace G. Healey. (Courtesy of Zaner-Bloser, Inc.)

Scalloped Miniature Roses

French shaded wire-edged ribbon makes each of this lesson's buds and roses, differing only in width, length, and color. For Patterns 36-39, each bud is made from a ⅝" x 3" length of ribbon.

1. *Rosebud for Patterns 36, 37, and 39*: Hold a ⅝" x 3½" shaded-wired ribbon vertically, dark edge on the right. At point (a) (1½" down on the left side) fold the bottom of the ribbon to the right, at a right angle. Pinch the last ½" of ribbon at point (b). Roll this pinch tightly toward yourself, three times. This forms the bud stem.

2. Roll the stem to the left three times. A full circle of the wire edging now tops this roll. With tweezers, grab the left side of the wire circle, tightening it clockwise, then pulling it forward and down to form the bud center.

3. Lift the ribbon down from the left of the bud and across to the right, so that its raw edge lies under your thumb. Pin, then tack the rose in place on the background cloth.

4. *Pattern 38's bud begins differently*: It is made from a ⅞" x 2½" ribbon that is folded lengthwise, so that the front selvage falls ⅛" below the back one. Complete the bud with Steps 1 through 3.

Fig. 84 Miniature Rosebud for Patterns 36-39

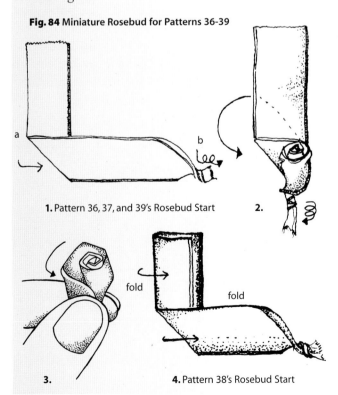

1. Pattern 36, 37, and 39's Rosebud Start

2.

3.

4. Pattern 38's Rosebud Start

Fig. 85 Miniature Scalloped Rose for Patterns 36 - 39

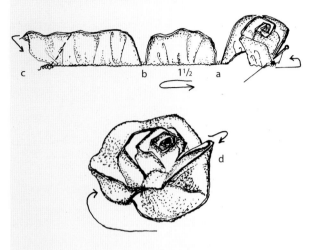

1. *Patterns 36, 37, and 39:* Hold a ⅝" x 15" length of shaded wired ribbon, dark edge on the right as in Figure 84. Insert a pin 6" up from the bottom. This marks the 6" needed to form the rose's bud center. Follow the bud-making Steps 1 through 3, pinning but not stitching the bud.

2. Gather the remaining 9" length by pulling the ribbon back on the bottom wire, toward the bud. Scrunch the wire into a knot (Figure 85, c) to hold the gathers.

3. Every 1½" left of the bud, twist the ribbon one full turn on the bottom wire to make three petals. Fold the finishing raw edge (c) to the gather edge at a 45° angle.

4. Wrap the length of the ribbon forward, across, then up and around behind the bud.

5. Thereafter, wrap the length back and forth across the bud's front until it is used up, in a roselike fashion (d).

6. After the pattern's leaves and stems are completed: Pin, then big-stitch baste the scalloped rose in place. Using a stab stitch just inside the wire edge, tack the rose to the background, tack-stitching all around from the bud center to its outer edges.

Pattern 38's rose is a ⅞" x 7" ribbon folded off-center lengthwise, so that the front selvage lies ⅛" below the back one. Roll the bud center as in Figure 84. Gather the remaining 5" on the fold at Step 2, then finish as above. Highlight the bud and rose stamens with a yellow Pigma Brush pen.

"Heart *en Cabochon* I" by Elly Sienkiewicz

Pattern 36
"Heart *en Cabochon* I"

PROCEDURE/APPLIQUÉ APPROACH

Pattern 36's (page 127) cut rose mixes UltraSuede appliqué, appliquéd silk ribbon leaves, and inkwork.

1. Cut out Pattern 36's fusible-backed blue heart center (page 127). Trace the rose foliage appliqué onto the blue, then heat-bond the heart to the background.
2. Stitch Pattern 36's cabochon frame (page 87).
3. Make contact paper templates for Pattern 36's UltraSuede leaves 1 through 5, and calyxes 6 and 7.
4. *UltraSuede appliqués*: Cut the calyxes and leaves, some out of one UltraSuede green, some of the other. Appliqué the leaves. Appliqué the sides and base of the layered calyx, leaving the top open to receive the bud.
5. *Silk ribbon leaf appliqués*: Gluestick both cut ends under (¼") on four 13mm x 1½" (a) ribbon lengths. Fold each corner of the hem in toward the center, shaping a crystal (b).
6. Baste one of these crystal-shaped silk ribbons, hem down (c), over leaf outlines 8, 9, 10, and 11.

7. The crystal will be too long for the leaf outline at first. Tack stitch it to conform; bring the needle up through the drawn line, then catch the ribbon's edge before re-entering at the same line.
8. When complete, the silk leaf's appliqué puffs in the center. With the same thread, make a center vein in running stitch (c), pulling the leaf down to the background.

Fig. 86 "Heart *en Cabochon* I," Pattern 36, leaf appliqué and embellishment details

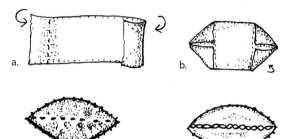

c. Silk ribbon leaf appliqué   d. UltraSuede leaf appliqué

9. Make Pattern 36's rose and bud (page 89). Stitch the bud into the calyx. Tack stitch the rose down.

EMBELLISHMENT

Outline Pattern 36's stems in black Pigma Micron 01 pen, adding color with a green Pigma Brush pen. With 3 strands of silk floss, crewel stitch all the leaves' center vein lines (d). With black Pigma Micron 01 pen, draw branching veins on the leaves, the smaller leaf veins and margin serrations (e), the moss around the rose (f), and the hairs on the stems (g).

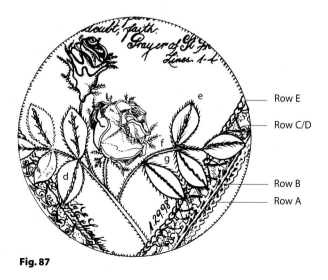

Fig. 87

"Heart *en Cabochon* II" by Elly Sienkiewicz

Pattern 37 "Heart *en Cabochon* II"

PROCEDURE/APPLIQUÉ APPROACH

Pattern 37's (page 127) rose mixes seamless appliqué with embroidery. To begin:

1. Cut out Pattern 36's fusible-backed heart (page 127). Use Pattern 38's rose foliage template to mark the appliqué placement on Pattern 37's heart background.
2. Heat-bond the marked blue heart center to the background.
3. Stitch its cabochon frame (page 87).
4. Trace Pattern 37's foliage onto the paper side of the fusible web. Iron the web to the wrong side of green calico. Cut the foliage out of the fusible-backed green calico.
5. Make Pattern 37's rose and bud (page 89). Stitch the bud in place. Stitch down the rose after the foliage is completed.
6. Heat-bond the foliage appliqué over the bud and onto blue background. Its rose is now facing in Pattern 38's direction.

EMBELLISHMENT

7. *Stems*: Stem stitch embroider the rose's lower stem in three strands of green cotton floss. Blanket stitch appliqué all the other stems and the calyx with one green sewing thread.
8. *Leaves*: Blanket stitch each leaf in either black Nymo or antique gold embroidery thread. Reverse the blanket stitch so the stitch legs lie over the blue background and point toward the tip of the leaf. This can be seen in Figure 86 (c). The length of the stitch can rest at the raw edge or just inside it. When it rests at the edge it covers any drawn line and marginally enlarges the leaf. When it rests just inside the edge it gives a lighter, more sophisticated look. Alternating these options works well.
9. *Rose moss:* Pen fine sprays of moss with black Pigma Micron 01 or 005. In antique gold embroidery thread, fly stitch embroider a bit more moss to highlight the inkwork.
10. *Bead-embroidered dew:* Stitch a clear seed bead inside the rose's cup.

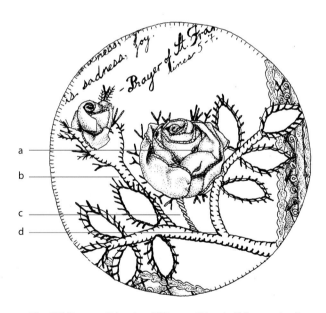

Fig. 88 "Heart en Cabochon II" Pattern 37, embellishment detail

Key: (**a**) Seed bead dewdrop
　　　(**b**) Blanket stitch
　　　(**c**) Stem stitch
　　　(**d**) Blanket stitch

"Heart *en Cabochon* III" by Elly Sienkiewicz

Pattern 38 "Heart *en Cabochon* III"

PROCEDURE/APPLIQUÉ APPROACH

Pattern 38's (page 127) rose mixes cutaway appliqué with embroidery. Because the cutaway is miniaturized it involves edge-sealing and more care. To begin:

1. Cut out Pattern 36's blue heart center (page 127). Mark it with Pattern 38's rose foliage appliqué, then heat-bond the marked heart to the background.

2. Stitch its cabochon frame (page 87).

3. Make a contact paper template for Pattern 38's rose foliage.

4. Stick the template to the right side of a swatch (not the cut out shape) of green calico.

5. Pin-pierce to align the templated swatch with the foliage marked on the background. Baste the left side of each stem through the paper. (The right sides are needleturned first.)

6. *Edge-sealing:* At template's edge, seal the green cloth's points, curves, and corners with clear nail polish. Cutting after the sealant has dried prevents fray on the finest seam allowances.

7. *Cutaway appliqué:* With #11 milliners needle and silk 100 thread, begin cutaway appliqué at (d) on the pattern, stitching from right to left. Try to bring your appliqué needle up through the drawn line of the background and then reinsert it back into that line. Review Cutaway

Appliqué (page 15) with particular attention to Miniaturization (page 20). Miniaturization reminds me of the schoolyard joke, "How do you dance with a porcupine?" with its wise rejoinder, "Carefully!"

8. Make Pattern 38's rose and bud (page 89). Stitch the bud in place, appliquéing the calyx's opening over it. Sew on the rose.

EMBELLISHMENT

Stem stitch the rose's stem and the bud's lower stem in silk buttonhole twist. Ink in the leaf serrations with black Pigma Micron 01 pen. Fly stitch the moss in sewing thread, using fine green and then a metallic gold thread.

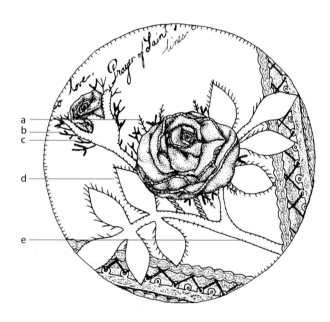

Fig. 89 "Heart *en Cabochon* III" Pattern 38, embellishment detail

Key: (a) Inked rose moss
(b) Embroidered rose moss
(c) Yellow Pigma pen highlight
(d) Inked leaf serrations
(e) Needleturn stem

"Heart *en Cabochon* IV" by Elly Sienkiewicz

Pattern 39 "Heart *en Cabochon* IV"

PROCEDURE/APPLIQUÉ APPROACH

Pattern 39's rose is a fancy combination of miniature onlaid needleturn, ribbon, and UltraSuede appliqué with embroidery. It has no pattern of its own and requires that you improvise. To begin:

1. For Pattern 39's rose foliage placement, trace Pattern 36 (page 127) onto the blue heart background. Heat-bond the heart center to the background, then stitch the heart's cabochon frame (page 87).

2. Make contact paper templates for Pattern 36's (page 127) leaves 2, 3, 4, 9, and 10. Make a template for the needleturned portion of the main rose stem. Stick these templates to the right side of green calico. Place the leaves and stem on the straight of grain. Carefully paint the seam allowance beyond the template with clear nail polish before cutting it a scant ⅛" wide.

3. **By needleturn, with contact paper template on top**: Pin-pierce to align the template edges with the background markings. Baste, then needleturn appliqué the leaves. Stitch the appliquéd cloth stem (k) finely, first its left side, top to bottom, then its right side, bottom to top, taking the last stitch twice. With the tip of your embroidery scissors, shove the top seam allowance down into

the stem tunnel and stitch across it. If you prefer, draw around each miniature appliqué with a fine black Pigma Micron 01 pen and remove the paper template before basting to the background.

4. **Ribbon boat leaves**: Cut two ⅝" x 1⅛" lengths of Mokuba Velvet Ribbon and two of the shaded rayon ribbon (vintage). Seal the cut edges with clear nail polish. Make four boat leaves (page 76), Tack stitch the vintage ribbon leaves to leaf outlines 5 and 11 and the velvet ones to outline 1 and 8.

5. Make a single calyx template, combining Pattern 36's templates 6 and 7. Cut the template shape out of green UltraSuede. Appliqué the sides and base of the layered calyx, leaving the top open to receive the bud.

6. Make Pattern 39's bud and rose. Stitch them into place, appliquéing the top of the calyx over the bud.

EMBELLISHMENT

Stem stitch the remaining stems (see Figure 90) in silk buttonhole twist. In the same silk, reverse buttonhole the needleturned leaf margins and fly stitch moss around the bud and blossom.

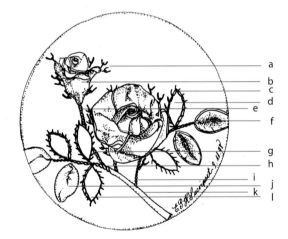

Fig. 90 "Heart *en Cabochon* IV" Pattern 39, embellishment detail

Key: (**a**) Fly-stitched rose moss in silk buttonhole twist
- (**b**) UltraSuede calyx
- (**c**) Blanket stitch (legs toward the background) embellishment in silk buttonhole twist
- (**d**) Green calico leaf by onlaid needleturn appliquéd
- (**e**) Stem stitch in silk buttonhole twist
- (**f**) Boat leaf in vintage rayon ribbon
- (**g**) Stem stitch in silk buttonhole twist
- (**h**) Stem stitch in silk buttonhole twist
- (**i**) Stem stitch in silk buttonhole twist
- (**j**) Boat leaf in Mokuba Velvet Ribbon
- (**k**) Green calico stem by onlaid needleturn appliqué
- (**l**) Green calico leaf by onlaid needleturn appliqué

Preface to PH.D. Honoris Causa

Lesson 10 sums up our lessons in fancy appliqué. As soon as its heart blocks were completed, I felt a loss. I had wanted to sew fish cut from silk, edges burnt black. I had wanted to simplify their forms into stylized patterns and explore how to create fish eyes and silk-embroidered fins. I had wanted to capture their watery habitat reflected by organdy overlays. I had wanted to pore over beautiful fishing books to understand the fisherman's devotion; had wondered if contemplative practice linked us—we fishers and quilters—for the world would seem a warmer place if this was true. So instead of ending our lessons here, I immersed myself in the blocks of Lesson 11 and 12 for a dozen days on end. Might we call such an esoteric exploration a Ph. D. in fine appliqué?

"Kenyan children are taught English in primary school," said my 19-year-old Katya, telling me about the semester in Kenya from which she had just returned. "Everywhere, we white students were stared at as exotics. When our lorry drove into rural areas, we burst onto the horizon like a truckload of marshmallows. At one village, a throng of kids ran toward us, shouting, '*Why* are you?' '*Why* are you?' '*Why* are you?' This, their take on '*How* are you?', set us a-giggle."

"*Why are you?*" I ask of myself. The question recurs. As a young adult, in awe of my father, a renowned physicist, I asked how it had come to be that his children were history and sociology majors with not a scientist among us. "As physics probes the nature of the universe, so history probes the nature of man," he replied thoughtfully. I loved him the more for his serious answer. It made me feel less lonely, as the meeting of souls always does. And why, fellow needlewomen, why are *we* quiltmakers?

Who of us asked "why?" when we learned to quilt? Our first questions were all "how?" The cloth and the craft called to us; we longed to learn it, we yearned for it. Did something unexpected—magic, even—then happen inside you when you became skillful? For me, *how* and *why* are now inseparable.

How rings a challenge. *Why* stitches the visible to the invisible. In rearranging cloth, my understanding also changes. Are the *how* and *why* also entwined for you? This is not a question we address routinely, we moderns. But here in the privacy of the printed word, let's explore stitchery and soul as friends who journey together. The postulate is this: The visible patterning of our appliqué aids the invisible patterning of our understanding. Like Abe Lincoln, who home-schooled in Law, might this not earn us a Doctor of Philosophy (*Honoris Causa*) in fine appliqué? And if thereby we gain skill and better understand why we are quiltmakers, what can be the harm in it? Listen for that question in answer to which you yourself will stitch a thesis. If you listen, the question—and the quilt—will come!

The eloquent man is he who is no beautiful speaker,
but who is inwardly and desperately drunk with
a certain belief.

—Ralph Waldo Emerson, *Journals*

LESSON 11

Mixed Media Appliqué and Scenery Blocks

I went out to the hazel wood,
Because a fire was in my head,
And cut and peeled a hazel wand,
And hooked a berry to a thread,
And when white moths were on the wing,
And moth-like stars were flickering out,
I dropped the berry in a stream
And caught a little silver trout.

—William Butler Yeats

When seven years of age, my first-born lay on our Severn River dock and stared into the water for hours. He knew snakes, turtles, and fish, and treated each with reverence. Now married, he and his wife and my second son are all catch-and-release fishermen. So I peruse books on the subject. My proposal was that I should research fishing in a pleasing way, reading naturalists' journals, and stitching sites encountered between those covers. The result is the water scenes of Lessons 11 and 12: their fish, a frog, and even a merman. My postulate (what a Ph.D. candidate calls a thesis) was: "There is a soul-satisfying commonality in the journey taken by fishermen and quilters." I argued that thesis in thread and, pleased with what I'd learned, thought it worth a Ph.D. in Appliqué, *honoris causa.* The next thesis I propose is: "By reading my father's favorite poet, William Wordsworth, and stitching fancywork thus inspired, I'll visit with my departed dad, and wrap his wisdom 'round me." If that thesis gets stitched, I might add another imaginary honorary degree after my name, for I gather there's no limit a needlewoman may earn!

Things that pass us, go somewhere else and don't come back,
seem to communicate directly with the soul. That the fisherman
plies his craft on the surface of such a thing possibly accounts for
his contemplative nature.

—Thomas McGuane, *Season of the Angler*

Materials

For basic supplies, see Appliqué Supplies, page 12.

PATTERN 40

Appliqué (Layer A): 6" scrap of hand-dyed sky blue fabric, fusible-backed; 2" wide x 4" scrap of Artemis bias-cut silk in Midas Touch, backed with Steam-a-Seam 2 fusible bonding web (repositionable adhesive on both sides); 3" x 12" (allows graded color choice) Mokuba Gradation Organdy Ribbon (#4881, 75mm, color 2).
Background (Layer B): 9" square of printed cotton

PATTERN 41

Appliqué (Layer A): 6" scrap of hand-dyed sky blue fabric, fusible-backed; *Trout:* 4" scrap of 2"-wide Artemis bias-cut silk in Flamingo Glacé, backed with Steam-a-Seam 2; *Lake scene:* 1½" (38mm) x 12" (allows graded color choice) in Mokuba Gradation Organdy Ribbon (#4881, color 2) overlay. Alternatively, to make the lake all one piece, use a 3" (75mm) ribbon. Ribbon Appliqué scraps of ribbons, backed with Steam-a-Seam 2: 1½"-wide shaded vintage or wired ribbon, 1½"-wide Artemis bias-cut silk in Moon Goddess, Electric Dancer, and Abalone; 1½" variegated green silk embroidery ribbon (also backed with Steam-a-Seam 2).
Background (Layer B): 9" square of printed cotton

PATTERN 42

Appliqué (Layer A): 6" scrap of hand-dyed sky-blue fabric, fusible-backed; *Ocean/lagoon:* Ribbon color 1 (3" x 6" length of Artemis bias-cut silk in Robin's Egg Blue); Organza color 2 (Mokuba Organdy Ribbon #1550, 75mm, color 63); Organza color 3 (Mokuba Gradation Organdy Ribbon #4881, 75mm, color 2); *Marlin:* 2" wide x 4" scrap Artemis bias-cut silk in Blue Jeans, backed with Steam-a-Seam 2; *Promontory rocks:* Ribbon Appliqué scraps all backed with Steam-a-Seam 2: 1½" wide Artemis bias-cut silk in Moon Goddess (narrow promontory rocks); Moon Dust (mid-ground); Misty (background); and Lobelia (foreground rocks).
Background (Layer B): 9" square of printed cotton

Supplies for Embellishment

PATTERN 40

Frame: ⅝" x 22" of Mokuba Velvet Ribbon (#2500, color 39); edge the velvet with 20" of gold Mokuba Beaded Yarn (#0140, color 34), ⅛" miniature yellow picot trim, clear colorless seed beads, and yellow silk buttonhole twist; *Pussy willows:* Stems are 2mm-wide UltraSuede, packaged as Needle Necessities UltraSuede Thread (loden green) or Mokuba Suede Tape (#1509, 2mm, color 16); a scrap of apple green UltraSuede for pussy willow calyxes; 4mm and 7mm green silk embroidery ribbon for pussy willow calyxes; 7mm dove color silk embroidery ribbon for pussy willow blossoms; ⁷⁄₁₆"-wide Artemis bias-cut silk in Moon Goddess; brown Pigma Micron 01 pen; *Trout:* gold metallic and orange sewing thread; 4mm variegated green silk embroidery ribbon; 7mm variegated yellow silk embroidery ribbon; colored pencils; Pigma Brush pens in yellow and green, Pigma Micron 01 and 005 pens in black; *Shore grass:* 2mm yellow braid; 7mm variegated yellow and green silk embroidery ribbon.

PATTERN 41

Trout: gold metallic sewing thread; 4mm silk embroidery ribbon in variegated green and red; black Pigma Micron 01 pen; colored pencil; *Frame:* Four ½" x 4½" strips of sandstone color UltraSuede; trims: miniature yellow picot trim; miniature 2mm-wide red braid and yellow braid; ¼"-wide beige looped trim; 3mm antique gold braid; gold seed beads; silver clear glass seed beads; *Lake:* edge-burned organza and gold thread.

PATTERN 42

Blue Marlin: 4mm variegated blue silk embroidery ribbon; antique gold embroidery thread; black Pigma Micron 01 pen; *Frame:* ⅝" x 24" vintage shaded rayon ribbon; 2mm red braid, ¼"-wide looped beige trim; *Rocks:* Brown and black Pigma Micron 01 pens and colored pencils.

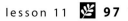

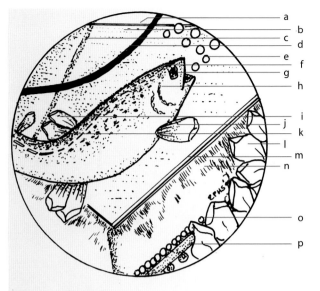

Fig. 91 Constructing Pattern 40's frame

Key :(a) The selvage of the organdy ribbon overlay is the waterline
(b) The organdy ribbon as water
(c) A pussy willow branch (UltraSuede Thread) lying underneath the organdy ribbon
(d) UltraSuede ribbon branch lying over the organdy ribbon
(e) Air bubble depicted by a clear glass seed bead
(f) A flame-burned edge of the silk trout appliqué
(g) Fish eye: gold metallic thread embroidery over black Pigma Micron 01 pen circle
(h) Gills embroidered in crewel stitch with a single sewing thread
(i) Pierced leaf stitch in variegated 4mm silk embroidery ribbon
(j) Pierced leaf stitch in variegated 7mm silk embroidery ribbon with embellishment in sewing thread crewel stitch and orange and green Pigma Brush pens
(k) Black Pigma Micron 005 pen over Pigma Brush pen in green and yellow
(l) Pierced leaf stitch in variegated 7mm silk embroidery ribbon
(m) Crewel stitch in silk buttonhole twist
(n) Mokuba Velvet Ribbon frame (#2500), ironed at random angles to crush and antique it
(o) Mokuba Beaded Yarn (#1040, color 34) gold bead cord couched with clear glass seed beads
(p) 3mm yellow picot trim

The Diamond Frames of Fancy Album II

For efficiency, prepare the four background squares for this lesson's Patterns 40, 41, 42, and Lesson 12's Pattern 43 at the same time. While these blocks quickly diverge, they only do so when the frames are put on, after the organdy ribbon overlay has created the illusion of water. To begin:

1. Trace Pattern 40's center diamond (Line A) and its framing diamond (Line B) onto each of four background squares.

2. Back a 12" x 12" scrap of variegated sky blue with lightweight fusible bonding. (Fusible bonding stiffens cloth much the way that a hoop aids embroidery.)

3. Cut out four fusible-backed sky blue center diamond shapes on Line B.

4. Heat-bond one diamond, centered, onto each background square.

5. Set up each block's appliqué in the following order: 1. Lay out the interior scene, then onlay its organdy ribbon; 2. Frame it with trim; and 3. Add the creature appliqué. The four blocks' scenes and creatures are taught block by block, but first we will learn their frame construction:

6. *The dominant trim*: Cut a ⅝" (15mm) x 22" length of Mokuba Velvet Ribbon (#2500, color 39) for the diamond frame. Start the ribbon with a 1" tail laid above the blue diamond's left-hand corner. Align the ribbon's inside edge with pattern line A. Baste the ribbon's outside edge with white glue on a toothpick. (Leave the ribbon frame's inside edge open until you tuck under the brook scene's organdy ribbon overlay.) Pin a miter-fold at the first ribbon corner. Repeat this process for three corners. When you return to the left-hand corner, miter-cut the ribbon tails and seal the raw edges with nail polish.

7. *Echo trim*: Glue-baste 20" of 3mm yellow picot trim to Figure 91's line, rounding its corners. When you come back around to its beginning, trim off the excess, nail polish-sealing the cut. Couch gold Mokuba Beaded Yarn over the picot trim's inside edge (at o), tacking every ¼" with a clear seed bead.

8. *Horizontal corners*: Cut two ⅝" x 2½" lengths of velvet ribbon, then fold and glue-baste their ends under to meet in the middle. Glue-baste, then appliqué these rectangles (raw edges down) to the frame's horizontal corners as pictured in the photo. When the velvet ribbon frame has been appliquéd, press it first one way and then the other way with the point of a steam iron to "antique" the velvet.

PATTERN 41'S FRAME

Glue-baste UltraSuede (overlapped at the corners, then miter-cut to abut) so that its inside edge lies just over Line B's raw edge. Under the fish and at Line A, begin and end four nested rows of trim. The rows are first (adjacent to the scene) a miniature yellow picot trim, second a miniature red braid, third a miniature yellow braid, then fourth the antique gold braid. As shown in the block's photo, the antique gold braid is curved into an oval at each corner. Miniature gold braid lined with a row of gold seed beads frames each oval and is filled with colorless seed beads. Outlining the UltraSuede frame's outer edge is antique gold braid framed by ¼"-wide looped beige trim. Both these trims also begin and end under cover of the fish. Inscribe the center diamond's UltraSuede frame with Thoreau's lake quote (page 128) in black Pigma Micron 01 pen.

PATTERN 42'S FRAME VARIATION

Pattern 42's pattern line A is bordered by ¼"-wide looped beige trim, mitered, and outlined with miniature red braid. Its outer frame is a ⅝" x 24" vintage rayon ribbon with miter-folded corners. The framing trims begin and finish under the marlin.

Caution: The vintage rayon ribbon should not be glue-basted because the glue may stain it.

PATTERN 43'S FRAME VARIATION

Pattern 43's five rows of trim all have rounded corners, all are glue-basted before sewing, and all begin and end hidden under the merman's tail. From inside to outside, the trim rows are: 3mm antique gold braid, 3mm yellow picot trim, 6mm red Mokuba Pleated Satin Ribbon (#0492, color 1), 3mm antique gold braid, and, at the outside, 3mm yellow picot trim. These can be glue-basted using a toothpick and white glue, then appliquéd down.

"Trout in Pussy Willow Time" by Elly Sienkiewicz

Pattern 40 "Trout in Pussy Willow Time"

PROCEDURE/APPLIQUÉ APPROACH

"Trout in Pussy Willow Time" explores organdy ribbon water and mixes the media of UltraSuede, silk and velvet ribbon, edge-burning, trims, gold threadwork, paint, colored pencil, and bead embroidery.

1. After heat-bonding Pattern 40's variegated blue diamond to the background cloth (page 128), rule in its high water mark.
2. Make a contact paper trout template and with it, draw the fish outline on the block. Pencil a single line for each main pussy willow branch.
3. Glue-baste, then appliqué the pussy willow stems (a), (b), (c), and (d) in Suede Thread.
4. With tiny running stitches, appliqué a 3" x 6" strip of organdy ribbon to the high water mark (and over pussy willow stems (a, b, c, and d). Trim the lower part of the ribbon into a "V" ⅜" deeper than the frame. Edge-seal the cut ribbon with clear nail polish. When dry, tuck the ribbon under the velvet and appliqué the velvet frame over it.
5. ***The brook trout***: Peel off the 2" x 4" swatch of Steam-a-Seam 2's non-printed backing, then press this self-stick fusible web to the wrong side of a 2" x 4" cut of Artemis bias-cut silk in Midas

Touch. Gently finger-press the contact paper trout cut-out to the right side of the silk, making a four-layer fish sandwich of contact paper, silk, fusible web, and the web's paper backing. Draw ever so lightly around the shape with a black Pigma Micron 005 pen. Then with embroidery scissors, cut the silk ¹⁄₁₆" bigger than the fish template all around. This ¹⁄₁₆" leaves a tiny margin for edge-burning.

EDGE-BURNING SILK

Light a low, stable candle (a votive candle is ideal). Hold the silk cut-out between thumb and forefinger of both hands. Keeping the shape horizontal so that you watch the process, pass the edge close to the flame. The edge will char and melt back. If it catches fire, quickly blow it out. Edge-burning fuses the silk's edge for stability. In addition, it outlines the silk with an attractive dark, hand-drawn looking line. After edge-burning the fish's perimeter, remove the contact paper from above the silk fish and the web's protective paper from underneath it. **Caution**: Please be careful not to burn your fingers!

6. Position the fish over Pattern 40's quilt square, fusible web down. Using a Teflon press sheet, heat-bond the fish to the background.

7. *Mixed media fish embellishment*: Lightly pencil the fish's anatomical details onto the silk shape. Go over the pencil marks in black Pigma Micron 005 pen. Crewel stitch the gills and mouth in a single orange thread (see Figure 91, h). Embroider the fins (i, j) in variegated 4mm and 7mm silk ribbon. Embroider the eye in metallic gold sewing thread. Running stitch the "shine line," highlighting the fish's glimmering back, with a single strand of gold sewing thread. Shade the back and belly with Pigma Brush pen and colored pencil. Pigma Micron pen-inked speckles (k) and seed bead bubbles (e) rising from his mouth finish the fish appliqué.

8. *Pussy willow time*: Appliqué the final Suede Thread willow stems (see Pattern 40, e and f), laying them over the velvet frame, organdy water, and trout tail.

9. With ³⁄₈" wide Artemis bias-cut silk in Moon Goddess, make a ½" deep loop (Figure 92, c) for many of the pussy willow blossoms. You can also use 7mm silk embroidery ribbon. Shape the blossom's top edge by appliqué. With 4mm green silk embroidery ribbon, pierced leaf stitch a calyx (e) or appliqué one in UltraSuede (a). Shade both blossoms and calyxes to greater dimension with Pigma Brush pen, darkening the calyx where it meets the stem with touches of brown Pigma Micron 01 pen.

10. By eye, straight-stitch embroider miniature yellow braid stems to form marsh brush at the block's lower right (f). Leaf them out with 7mm silk ribbon, pierced leaf stitched.

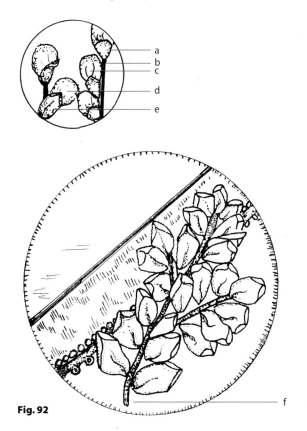

Fig. 92

Key: Pattern 40's Flora

  (**a**) UltraSuede calyx, colored pencil and ink embellished

  (**b**) Suede Thread stem

  (**c**) Bias silk ribbon (loop-stitched and appliquéd across the top)

  (**d**) 7mm silk embroidery ribbon loop-stitched and appliquéd into a curve at the top

  (**e**) Pierced leaf stitched calyx in 4mm variegated silk embroidery ribbon

  (**f**) Miniature yellow braid stems of marsh brush

"Lake Trout Spring" by Elly Sienkiewicz

Pattern 41 "Lake Trout Spring"

Thoreau's words are inscribed on this block's frame (page 128). This square teaches a wondrously simple miniature landscape technique using mirror-imaged ribbon appliqués.

PROCEDURE/APPLIQUÉ APPROACH

Constructing the Scene

1. After heat-bonding this square's blue diamond center (page 40), rule the lake's shoreline (a).
2. Using contact paper templates, cut Pattern 41's (page 128) hills (b) and mountains (c) out of Artemis bias-cut silk and shaded ribbon in Green Apple, Tuscany, and Robin's Egg. Cut each unit double. Edge-burn the exposed edges (page 99), double.
3. By eye, place the hills and mountains above the shoreline. The Steam-a-Seam 2's film of glue will hold them temporarily in place. Lay out their reflection, mirror-imaged, below the shoreline.
4. Fold a strip of fusible-backed green silk in half lengthwise (right sides together) for the shoreline's greenery (d). Finger-press to crease the fold, then (from the fusible web side) running stitch a tuck ⅛" parallel to—and along the

length of—the fold. Cut the greenery hill and valley shape, then edge-burn the shape, double.
5. With a press cloth, iron the green shoreline tuck's seam to the drawn shoreline. Press the tuck's seam allowances upward as you heat-bond the green silk foothills (b) and mountains (c) at the same time. No further appliqué is needed.
6. With pen and colored pencils, shade the hills, mountains, and sky for more drama. Shade the landscape both above the water and in its mirror image below.
7. Lay a 1½"-wide Mokuba Gradation Organdy Ribbon from the scene's seamed shoreline on down. Baste, then tack stitch its upper edge to the shoreline. A second piece of organdy fills in the bottom of the scene. Edge-burn its left side for interest. (Alternatively, use a single 3"-wide cut of ribbon.) Draw glints on the water with running stitch in gold thread.
8. Make Pattern 41's trout as you did in Pattern 40 (page 98). Embroider the trout's eye in gold metallic thread.
9. Complete the square by heat-bonding its luscious trout in place.

"Blue Marlin off Patagonia" by Elly Sienkiewicz

Pattern 42
"Blue Marlin off Patagonia"

My younger fisherman, Alex Corbly Sienkiewicz, spent several months mountain climbing in Patagonia, Chile, and reports that the coast there looks like that in this block. Its scene builds on the techniques used for Pattern 41, but is more complex. Its focus is the middle picture plane, a promontory jutting out into the ocean. The back picture plane shows the distant horizon while a rocky foreground defines the front picture plane.

PROCEDURE/APPLIQUÉ APPROACH

1. Begin Pattern 42 (page 129) by heat-bonding the blue diamond to the background. Pencil in the horizon (a).
2. Appliqué the top edge of ribbon Color 1 to the horizon. Appliqué Organza Color 2's top edge beginning ¹⁄₁₆" below and lying parallel to ribbon Color 1.
3. *Promontory and pines*: The promontory, or headland (three shapes cut from fusible-backed bias-cut silk, edge-burned and heat-bonded over ribbon Colors 1 and 2) is repeated below, upside down in reflection. (Construct the mirror image as in Steps 2 to 4 in Pattern 41, placing the folded and stitched shoreline ribbon at the waterline and layering Pattern 42's template-cut landmasses both above and below it.) Embellish the foremost promontory rocks with ink and colored pencils. Underline them with a single antique gold embroidery thread, couched. Steam-a-Seam 2's imprint may show through the silk in places, adding texture. Pencil, then straight stitch the trees to scale, embroidering them with a single sewing thread. Do this mixed media embellishment above and below the shoreline before Organza Color 3's lagoon is appliquéd down.
4. *The foreground rocks* are Artemis bias-cut silk, edge-burned and heat-bonded over the organza ocean.
5. *The marlin's fabrication* echoes that of the trout in Pattern 41, and like the trout, she goes on last.

LESSON 12

Stumpwork ~
A Fancywork Crescendo

How dreary — to be — Somebody!
How public — like a Frog —
To tell one's name — the livelong June —
To an admiring Bog!

—Emily Dickinson (1861)

Stumpwork is "elaborate raised embroidery of the fifteenth to seventeenth centuries using various materials, and raised by stumps of wood or pads of wool," reads the *Twentieth Century Dictionary*. Some hypothesize that the Stumpwork era was more protracted, or that the word "stumpwork" (*stumpfwerk* in German) originated as work on a stamped background. While Stumpwork is a controversial embroidery term, it can refer to a worked foundation cloth, which is cut to shape and then appliquéd over a dense form onto background cloth. Popular today among Commonwealth embroiderers, the art's free-spirited dimensionality intrigues me as a quiltmaker. Its raised wired petals, for instance, differ dramatically from a quilt's softly functional attributes. Still, Stumpwork Appliqué (to coin a term) could explore Stumpwork embroidery's engineering, accept its invitation to mixed media, and emulate its sculptural elevation from an undistorted foundation cloth. These possibilities inspired this lesson's aquatic creatures.

Materials

For basic supplies, see Appliqué Supplies, page 12.

PATTERN 43
Appliqué (Layer A): 6" scrap of hand-dyed sky blue fabric, fusible-backed. (See The Diamond Frames of Fancy Album II, page 97, to make Pattern 43's frame.) ***The scene***: (a) 1½" x 6" Artemis bias-cut silk in Pine Needle; (b) ¼" x 3" green with gilt-edged "lettuce" ruffle trim; (c) 1½" x 4" Artemis bias-cut silk in Mocha Mint; (d) 1½" x 4" Artemis bias-cut silk in Terrazzo; ***The water overlay***: Mokuba Gradation Organdy Ribbon #4881, 75mm x 18" length to allow for color choice; ***Bow and arrow***: Scraps of wine and salmon colored UltraSuede; miniature red braid; 1mm-wide loden green UltraSuede tape for arrow; ***Merman***: Scraps of fawn and rose colored

UltraSuede; 1½" x 6" vintage shaded rayon ribbon; ***Goldfish and heart***: 1½" x 4" Artemis bias-cut silk in Valentino, backed with Steam-a-Seam 2; scraps of red and white UltraSuede.
Background (Layer B): 9" square of printed cotton

PATTERN 44
Appliqué (Layer A): 6" scrap of hand-dyed sky blue fabric, Steam-a-Seam 2-backed. ***Frog***: Scraps of UltraSuede in dark, medium, and light green for body and black for eyes; scrap of thin, dense cotton batting such as Warm and Natural; ***Branch***: Overdyed chenille yarn (Quilter's Resource, Chicago, #4028, Olive/wine) adhered to a Steam-a-Seam 2 log shape.
Background: 9" square of printed cotton

Supplies for Embellishment

PATTERN 43

7 mm and 4mm silk embroidery ribbon for merman's tail and foliage; scrap of thin, dense cotton batting; hand-dyed variegated, yellow size 5 pearl cotton for hair; metallic gold sewing thread; orange sewing thread; clear, colorless seed bead; silk 100 thread; Pigma Micron 005 and 01 pens in red, brown, and black; Pigma Brush pens; colored pencils.
(For Pattern 43's frame embellishment supplies, see Lesson 11's Materials, page 96.)

PATTERN 44

Frame: 2mm antique gold braid; antique gold and antique silver embroidery threads; seed beads in silver, bronze, deep berry purple; cotton and silk flosses in purple, green, and beige; 2mm, 4mm and 7mm silk embroidery ribbon from Jenifer Buechel and The Thread Gatherer (see Sources, page 140); yellow braid; black Pigma Micron 005 and 01 pens; green and yellow Pigma Brush pens; colored pencils; scraps of dense, thin cotton batting; (toilet) tissue paper; silk 100 thread; ⅝"-wide vintage rayon ribbon; 15mm Mokuba Luminous Ribbon (#4586, color 7); 8mm Mokuba Organdy Ribbon (#1500, color 26); ⅝"-wide gold-edged spark organdy ribbon (PON 6944m from Quilter's Resource); ⅝"-wide Artemis bias-cut silk in African Violet; one 6 x 9mm plastic pony bead. For the remaining embellishments referenced in the block's pattern layout and colored photo, see "A Wreath Lush with Fancywork," page 105.

"Time is the Stream I Go A-Fishing In" by Elly Sienkiewicz

Pattern 43 "Time is the Stream I Go A-Fishing In"

PROCEDURE/APPLIQUÉ APPROACH

"Time is the stream I go a-fishing in," wrote Henry David Thoreau. The words, the plump merman bow-fishing, the elusive goldfish, and the heart-shaped bubble inscribed "Mother" (for mine) all came together in this block which, appropriate to mothers and daughters, is magically mysterious. Where did Thoreau fish? In the past? The present? The future? And you? "Don't take it serious," my Mom would rhyme, "Life's too mysterious." Lit only by the moon, this scene's stream suggests more questions than answers.

1. Mark the merman, bow, arrow, and shoreline onto Pattern 43's (page 129) blue diamond Layer A.
2. The scene's edge-burned topography and its reflection are made the same way as for Pattern 41 (page 100, Steps 2 through 6). This scene's unique touches are pierced leaf stitches in silk ribbon embroidery and a gilt-edged ruffled ribbon called "lettuce." Both embellishments occur behind the merman's left arm.

3. Protected by a Teflon press cloth, iron the scene to heat-bond it to the background.

4. Tack a 3" x 6" piece of Mokuba Organdy Ribbon to the shoreline. It will overlay the foreground, washing it with shimmery water.

5. Add the diamond's frame border (page 97).

6. *The bright goldfish* is cut from Artemis bias-cut silk in Valentino, then heat-bonded to appear as if swimming beyond the frame, perhaps pursuing the red UltraSuede heart. The goldfish is made like Pattern 40's seamless appliqué fish (page 128). Appliqué its eyes in UltraSuede with black Pigma Micron pen-inked pupils. In crewel stitch with a single orange sewing thread, outline where the dorsal fin and tail join the body. Pen-shade the fish in fine red and brown Pigma Micron pen dots.

The Merman: This mythical creature has a vintage rayon ribbon lower body, with pierced leaf stitched tail in 4mm silk embroidery ribbon. His human upper body is padding-sculpted UltraSuede with inked, appliquéd, and embroidered features. To begin:

1. From contact paper, cut templates for the body, bow, and arrowhead. With the body template (protective paper left on), cut the body shape out of batting, cutting it down further by ⅛" all around. Glue-stick this padding to the merman drawn on the block.

2. Cut the whole body (full tail included) out of UltraSuede with a ¹⁄₁₆" margin (loft allowance) added beyond the paper template all around. In addition:

    Cut the pattern-marked arm/hand slit in the UltraSuede to allow for more dimension. (The right forearm will be appliquéd forward, fractionally overlapping its upper arm.)

    Cut the right hand free of the body. (It will be appliquéd over the arrow's hilt.)

    Slit the UltraSuede at the chin, cutting ½" along the arrow's shaft. (The head will be heavily stuffed and its chin appliquéd down for a convex effect. The resulting gap between chin and shoulder will be disguised by the arrow's shaft.)

3. Before appliqué, further stuff the upper body by glue-sticking shaped batting to forearms, palms, head, and torso. A second, and even a third batting shape (each trimmed back a bit more than the last) can be glued to the wrong side of the UltraSuede shape to build up the tummy, chest, head, and forehead/cheek area. This is like spreading the peanut butter and the jelly on the top piece of bread before you flop it over onto the bottom piece (the marked outline layered with one batting shape).

4. Big-stitch baste the UltraSuede body to its drawn outline, then appliqué it with fine silk, taking tiny stitches, each forcing the appliqué to fit the marked background. Cut back on the stuffing if distortion occurs—but an amazing amount fits. Take tiny stab stitches in silk 100 thread to sculpt indentations defining the stomach and breasts.

5. Cut a tail overlay (with a full ½" margin added beyond the template all around) of shaded vintage rayon ribbon. Seal the ribbon's cut edges with clear nail polish. For control, leave the paper template on the ribbon cut-out until the tail's appliqué and embroidery are finished. Pierced leaf stitch embroider the tip of the tail in variegated 4mm silk ribbon. Shade the lower tail with Pigma Brush pen to emphasize its twist.

6. Cut an UltraSuede bow and arrowhead. String the bow with miniature red braid inserted with a large needle. Appliqué UltraSuede Thread arrow shank.

7. Appliqué UltraSuede cheeks and embroider a mass of French knot curls done in two colors of size 5 pearl cotton. For finishing touches, add the inked features (facial and other anatomical details on fish and merman) and the Thoreau quote above the left border. Heat-set the ink with a fine press cloth.

A Wreath Lush with Fancywork

Pattern 44's courageous amphibian peers out from a stitched fairyland of flora. Here is the Key to the foliage, reading the pattern's layout numbers (page 130) clockwise, from the frog's left hand:

1. The stem is two strands of embroidery floss, crewel stitched. The pierced leaf stitched leaves are hand-dyed 7mm silk ribbon.

2. A spray of fly stitch branches with lazy daisy stitches in antique gold embroidery thread looked weak, so it has been embroidered over in the same manner as stem 1, but with leaves of 2mm silk ribbon. A bit of the antique gold lazy daisy stitch peeks through. Two twisted tendril stitches (page 41) in 4mm silk embroidery ribbon lie over the wreath frame.

3. Make stems of 2mm yellow braid. Make leaves of 7mm silk embroidery ribbon loop-stitched and appliquéd across the fold. Embellish with 4mm green silk-ribbon French knots and stamens inked with green and yellow Pigma Brush pen.

4. The stem is three strands of floss crewel-stitch embroidered. Like those on stem #2, the leaves are a longer pierced leaf stitch in 2mm silk embroidery ribbon. They look like sword ferns.

5. Same as #4, but the leaves are stitched in 7mm silk ribbon. Bunches of grape colored seed bead berries hang over the wreath's frame. These can be bead-embroidered with up to five beads threaded onto the needle at a time, then couched.

6. Boat leaves (page 76) in ⅝"-wide vintage rayon ribbon. Lazy daisy stitches in the background are embroidered in antique gold and antique silver embroidery thread. The berries are ¼" circles in UltraSuede appliqué accented by an antique silver French knot.

7. Same as Step 1.

8. Fine gold braid stem, tacked down, with pierced leaf stitch in 4mm silk embroidery ribbon.

9. Seed bead grape bunches, silk embroidery ribbon French knots, and tendril stitch lead to #9, which is the same as #2.

10. Same as Step 3, but a row of four silver seed bead daisies line the frame between 10 and 11.

11. The stems are three strands of floss, crewel-stitch embroidered with 15mm of Mokuba Luminous Ribbon (#4586, color 7) in pierced leaf stitch. French knots and matte finished seed beads nestle in the crooks of the stems.

12. The stems are three strands of floss, crewel-stitch embroidered with pierced leaf stitched 8mm Mokuba Organdy Ribbon (#1500, color 36).

13. The stem arc is crewel stitched (two strands of silk floss in the same needle with a single antique gold embroidery thread). The leaves are 4mm silk embroidery ribbon, lazy daisy stitched and highlighted with a Pigma Brush pen in yellow.

14. The stem is three strands of floss, crewel-stitch embroidered. The leaves are pierced leaf stitched in 4mm overdyed silk embroidery ribbon. Between #13 and #14, seven bell-like flowers intermingle with clusters of antique gold seed beads. Each bell flower is made of a ⅝" x 2¼" length of gold-edged spark organdy ribbon, sewn as in Figure 93, stuffed with tissue, gathered closed just inside the lip, then tacked to the background. Some of the flowers are double layered from a ⅝" x 4½" ribbon.

15. The stems and leaves are the same as #11. The bell flower is made with a bias-cut silk ribbon (Artemis, ⅝" wide in African Violet) sewn over a large plastic bead.

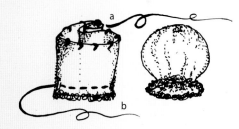

Fig. 93 Bell-like flowers: A ribbon length has French (or enclosed) seam folded to the back. Its top is whip stitched (a) and pulled into a tight cap. Tissue is stuffed to fill the bell, then a running stitch (b) is taken ⅛" above the bottom opening and pulled tightly to gather.

"Never Give Up, Never Give In" by Elly Sienkiewicz

Pattern 44 "Never Give Up, Never Give In"

"Never Give Up, Never Give In" was inspired by a naturalist's photo, by Annemieke Mein's nature drawings and mixed media machine needleart (*The Art of Annemieke Mein*)[1], and by two generations of mothers:

Born in 1915 to a Victorian mother, my mother was brought up on tales of fairies. She was a tomboy and pulled toward more rough and tumble things. When, overnight, a circle of mushrooms sprang up on our dew-wet front lawn, she named it a fairy circle. She had as a child, she said, been told how fairies congregated amongst such mushrooms. The way it was related, you knew she thought it impossible that anyone credit such malarkey (though in all fairness, I was taught to believe in Santa Claus). At five, I was fascinated by the mushroom ring and wanted to hear more about the "little people," but her heart was not in it. I came to understand that the fairies were part of her own mother's world; her exotic, unpredictable mother who in all ways was fancy.

So instead of drawing fairies, I cast deer and raccoon tracks in plaster, and as a first grader packed mud and grass into a cereal bowl seeking to replicate a robin's nest. Would my bird-expert teacher think it was real, I wondered? A professional artist, my mother stylized plants, people, and animals with a beautiful realism. I understood the world of her imagination better when she made an elegant model of the Life Cycle of the Garden Snail. She cut brown sandpaper into graceful curves of earth and glued on pearl-bead snail eggs to teach a Sunday School class called "How Miracles Abound." It made me wish I were in her class. So to my grandmother's fairy world, which still calls, and to my mother's love of nature's magic, this frog is dedicated.

1. Mein, Annemieke, *The Art of Annemieke Mein*, Search Press Limited, Turnbridge Wells, Kent. UK, 1994.

To make it:

1. Trace Pattern 44's (page 130) frog and branch to the blue center circle, backed with Steam-a-Seam 2. The Steam-a-Seam is a bit hard to stitch through but keeps the foundation cloth from distorting.

2. Heat-bond this circle to the foundation fabric.

3. Trace the 15 stem lines encircling Pattern 44's frame onto the foundation fabric.

4. Outline the central circle (Figure 94, g) with a row of 3mm antique gold braid. Crewel stitch two rows of antique silver embroidery thread around its outside, and a single row of antique gold embroidery thread crewel stitched around its inside. Embroider the curlicues (p) by caught-thread stitch in antique silver embroidery thread.

5. With a contact paper template (protective paper left on), cut the frog's body (Pattern 44, A) out of a fine dense batting, cutting just at the edge of the template. Gluestick-baste the batting to the frog's outline drawn on the blue background.

6. Remove the contact paper's backing and cut the frog body unit (A) out of the darkest green UltraSuede used. As you cut the frog body, add ¹⁄₁₆" all around the template to cover the batting without distortion. Body unit (A) includes the main body, the legs, and the left foot. Cut out the feet (B, D) and hands (C) and (E) out of the same dark green. Draw the outline of units (a), (b), (c), (d), and (e) onto the UltraSuede body unit (A). Use a black Pigma Micron 005 pen for ease and visibility.

7. Appliqué the full legs and body over the padded base, stitching in and out of the marked background lines, tucking under the batting as you stitch.

8. *Sandwich units*: Over the basic frog body, appliqué five "sandwich units": the bright green stomach (c), the pair of thighs (b) and (d) and the pair of calves (a) and (e), all visible in the photo. Make the stomach first to learn the process, then repeat it for each of the other units.

9. *The stomach*: Cut contact paper template c-1 out of medium green UltraSuede, cutting at the paper's edge. Cut c-2 out of a shade lighter apple green UltraSuede, cutting with a ¹⁄₁₆" margin beyond the template's edge to allow loft for stuffing. With template c-1, cut three layers of low, dense batting. Cut the bottom layer ⅛" smaller all around than the template and gluestick it, centered, onto c-1's UltraSuede cut-out (right-side up). Cut the second and third layers together, both ⅛" smaller than the first layer. Fold each of these layers in half lengthwise and gluestick them side-by-side to the first batting layer. (Putting them down side-by-side means that when you quilt the stomach line into this sandwich you'll sculpt this indented shape easily.) Gluestick the c-2 UltraSuede cut-out, centered, top of the sandwich. Appliqué c-2 finely in silk 100 thread, forcing it to fit within c-1 so that when finished, it is outlined by a ¹⁄₁₆" rim of c-1's medium green. Next, quilt the stomach sandwich, stitching the pattern's dotted line. Finally, gluestick-baste, then appliqué, the entire sandwiched stomach unit to the body. Next, sandwich the thighs with two batting layers, and the calves with a single batting layer. This is Stumpwork appliqué in action! The idea is not to distort the background but to achieve dramatic dimensionality nonetheless.

10. *Frog face*: UltraSuede appliqué the frog's black eyes. Optionally, pre-pad each eye with a smaller layer of UltraSuede. Embroider an antique silver French knot highlight on each eye. Crewel-stitch embroider a three strand line of floss for the mouth and around the eyes. Echo-stitch the mouth with a different shade of floss. With 4mm silk embroidery ribbon, take two satin stitches for the nostrils.

11. *The branch*: Cut Steam-a-Seam 2 to the pattern's branch shape. Press it to the blue cloth (and over the frog), then remove its second protective paper. Lay hand-dyed chenille yarn to cover it. Iron to heat-bond, then couch the yarn a bit.

12. Gluestick-baste, then appliqué the frog's hands and feet.

13. *Skylights*: With fine colored pencils, lighten the sky behind the frog. Use the side of the point to shade. The white, pink, yellow, and orange shades I used give our frog a magical aura and add depth to the background as well. Finish by embellishing the frog in fine amphibian inkwork, shading with dots done in black Pigma Micron 005 and 01 pen.

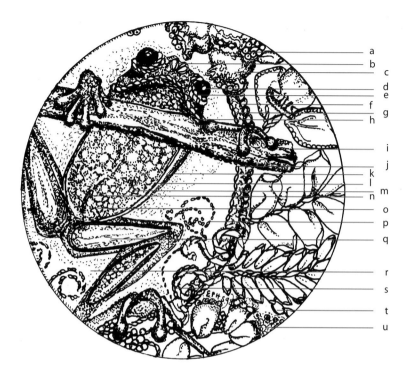

Fig. 94 Key: **(a)** Seed bead-embellished mouth of a bell flower

(b) Satin stitched silk ribbon embroidered nostrils

(c) Spark organdy ribbon bell flower

(d) Black UltraSuede eye

(e) Crewel stitch outlining the eye

(f) Double row of antique silver embroidery thread, crewel stitched, outlining the central trim

(g) 3mm antique gold braid stitched onto the drawn circle

(h) Crewel stitched mouth

(i) Branch fashioned from overdyed chenille yarn bonded to the blue cloth by Steam-a-Seam 2

(j) Single row of crewel stitch in antique gold embroidery thread lining the central trim

(k) Frog's UltraSuede body Layer A

(l) Frog's body Layer C (composed of c-1 and c-2 sandwiched with batting in between and appliquéd to outline C)

(m) Top layer of underbody C

(n) Quilted stomach line

(o) Skin detail drawn with black Pigma Micron 005 pen

(p) Antique silver embroidery thread in caught-thread stitch

(q) Top layer of thigh (units d-1 and d-2 sandwiched with batting in between and appliquéd to outline d)

(r) An aura created by colored pencil shading surrounds the frog

(s) Tendril stitch in 4mm silk embroidery ribbon, outlined by crewel stitch in antique silver embroidery thread

(t) A bit of the underlying foliage in antique gold embroidery thread (fly stitch and lazy daisy stitch) shows through

(u) 7mm silk embroidery ribbon, loop-stitched, appliquéd to a curved finish, topped by 4mm silk embroidery ribbon French knots with green and yellow Pigma Brush pen embellishments beyond

Finis

Follow your fancywork. It's good for the spirit and, sayeth our foremothers, it's good for the soul!

How blest the Maid whom circling years improve
Her God the object of her warmest love
Whose active years successive as they glide
The Book, the Needle, and the Pen divide.

—Anonymous nineteenth century needlework inscription

Part III

The Pattern Section

Fancy Appliqué's Two Sampler Album Quilts and forty-four lesson blocks are patterned here. A registration mark (crossed lines) at the center of each pattern guides placement. Symmetrical patterns must be traced on the top half of a square of folded contact or freezer paper. Staple the two halves together (stapling inside the drawn shape) then cut out double. Remove the staples and open the pattern to full size.

Note: Contact paper is cited as template material throughout *Fancy Appliqué* because it is particularly easy to use and find; however, freezer paper can be substituted for self-stick paper. Using a hot (linen setting) dry iron and a bread board upon which to iron, press the shiny side of the freezer paper to the right side of the appliqué cloth. Press heavily to temporarily bond freezer paper and fabric. The exceptions are UltraSuede, silk, and polished cotton, where you must press lightly and sometimes even to the wrong side of the cloth.

Block Preparation

1. Crease-mark its center. Fold the 9" background square into quarters.
2. Match the appliqué's center to the cloth's creased center by pin-piercing.

Pattern Transfer

When a pattern must be traced onto the background cloth to mark appliqué placement, it is noted in each lesson under Materials. One way to mark the background is to trace over a light box. Another is to trace the appliqué motif onto contact paper, cut it out, then trace the template's outline onto the background cloth. Adhere (gluestick, pin, or baste) the appliqué shapes over the shape drawn on the background. In a complex pattern, sew the first appliqué before introducing the second one, etc., rather than basting all at once.

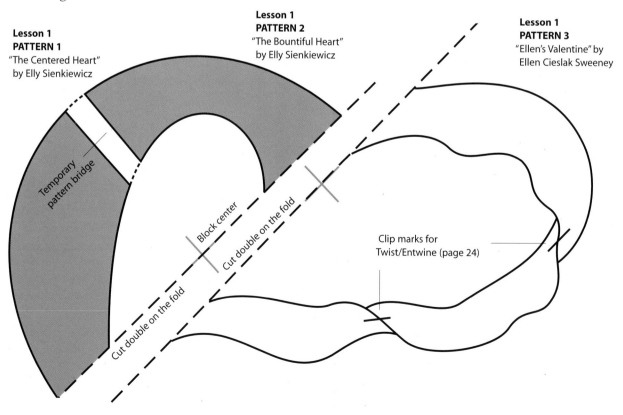

Lesson 1
PATTERN 1
"The Centered Heart"
by Elly Sienkiewicz

Lesson 1
PATTERN 2
"The Bountiful Heart"
by Elly Sienkiewicz

Lesson 1
PATTERN 3
"Ellen's Valentine" by
Ellen Cieslak Sweeney

Temporary pattern bridge

Block center

Cut double on the fold

Cut double on the fold

Cut double on the fold

Clip marks for
Twist/Entwine (page 24)

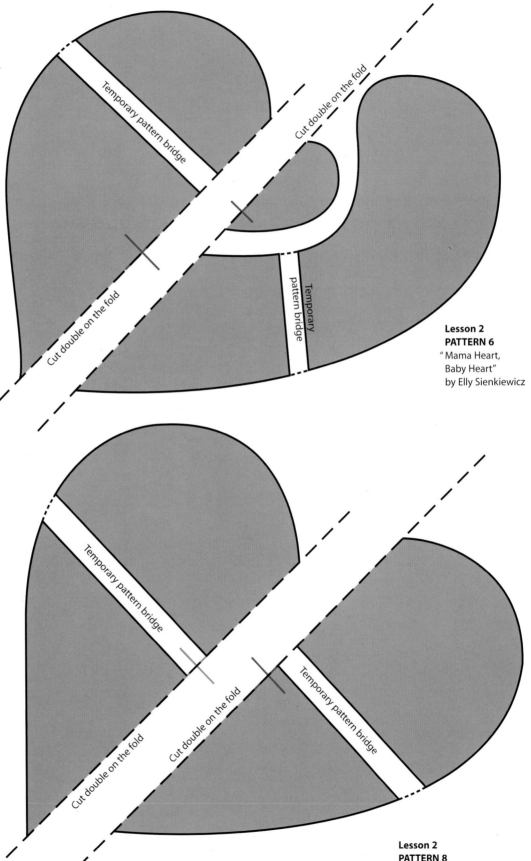

Lesson 2
PATTERN 4
"The Hurry-Up Heart"
by Elly Sienkiewicz
PATTERN 5
"Ribbon Collage Heart"
by Elly Sienkiewicz
Use Pattern 4 heart,
but center it on the
diagonal of the block
rather than the
vertical

Temporary pattern bridge

Cut double on the fold

Cut double on the fold

Temporary
pattern bridge

Lesson 2
PATTERN 6
"Mama Heart,
Baby Heart"
by Elly Sienkiewicz

Lesson 2
PATTERN 7
"Heart on the Edge"
by Elly Sienkiewicz
Lesson 4
PATTERN 15
"Roses of my Heart"
by Janet Cochran; and
Lesson 6
PATTERN 22
"Home Is
Where the Heart Is"
by Rosalie Schmidt

Temporary pattern bridge

Cut double on the fold

Cut double on the fold

Temporary pattern bridge

Lesson 2
PATTERN 8
"Sadie Rose" by Karan Flansha

Key: (See Embroidery
Primer on pages 30-31
for stitch instructions.)

Lazy daisy leaves

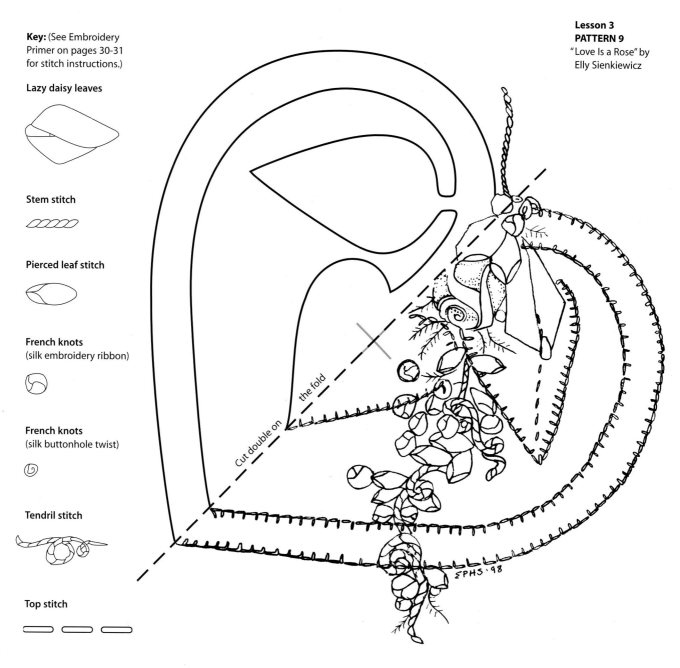

Stem stitch

Pierced leaf stitch

French knots
(silk embroidery ribbon)

French knots
(silk buttonhole twist)

Tendril stitch

Top stitch

Blanket stitch

Wired-edge ribbon rose

Fern

Cut double on the fold

Lesson 3
PATTERN 10
"Love is Mom"
by Elly Sienkiewicz

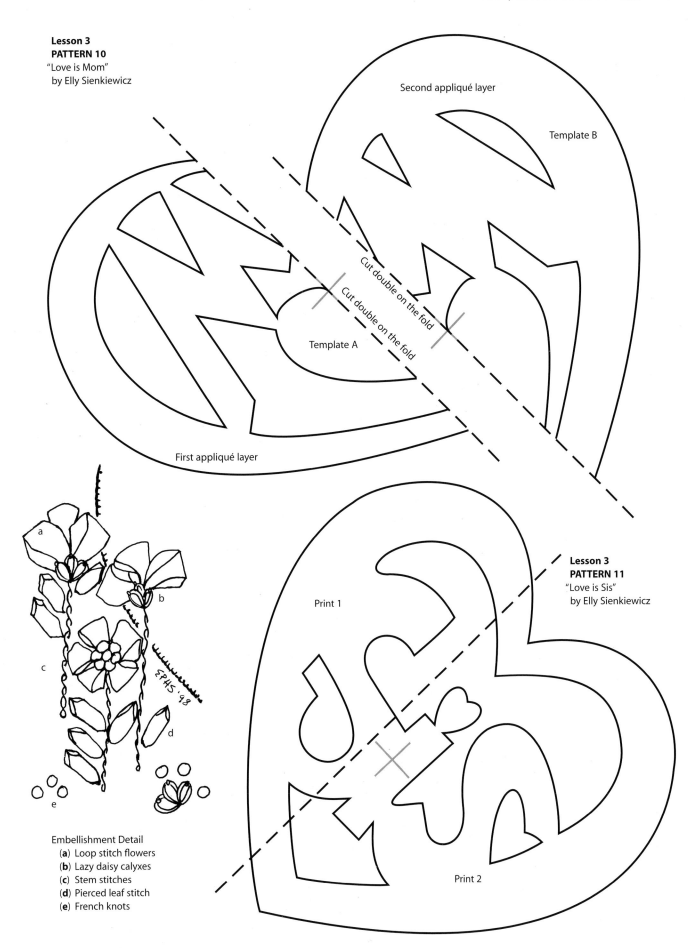

Second appliqué layer

Template B

Cut double on the fold

Cut double on the fold

Template A

First appliqué layer

Lesson 3
PATTERN 11
"Love is Sis"
by Elly Sienkiewicz

Print 1

Print 2

Embellishment Detail
(**a**) Loop stitch flowers
(**b**) Lazy daisy calyxes
(**c**) Stem stitches
(**d**) Pierced leaf stitch
(**e**) French knots

Cut double on the fold

Cut double on the fold

**Lesson 4
PATTERN 12**
"Filigreed Heart"
by Susan Gilbert

Embroidery
line only

**Lesson 4
PATTERN 13**
"Doves in Love"
by Elly Sienkiewicz

Crewel stitch
edge-embroidery

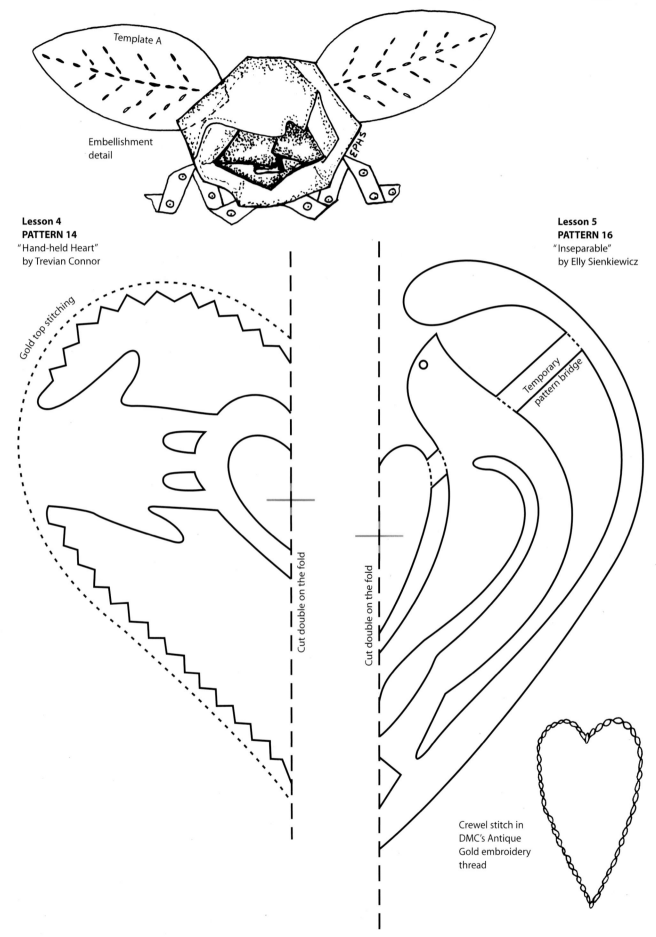

Template A

Embellishment
detail

EPHS

Lesson 4
PATTERN 14
"Hand-held Heart"
by Trevian Connor

Lesson 5
PATTERN 16
"Inseparable"
by Elly Sienkiewicz

Gold top stitching

Temporary
pattern bridge

Cut double on the fold

Cut double on the fold

Crewel stitch in
DMC's Antique
Gold embroidery
thread

Lesson 5
PATTERN 17
"Love in Bloom"
by Rosalie Schmidt

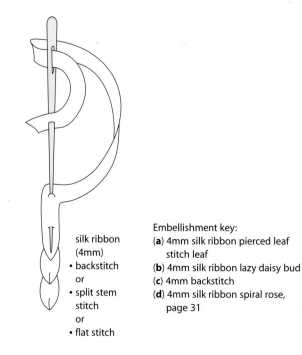

silk ribbon
(4mm)
• backstitch
or
• split stem
stitch
or
• flat stitch

Embellishment key:
(**a**) 4mm silk ribbon pierced leaf
stitch leaf
(**b**) 4mm silk ribbon lazy daisy bud
(**c**) 4mm backstitch
(**d**) 4mm silk ribbon spiral rose,
page 31

Heart and leaf appliqués

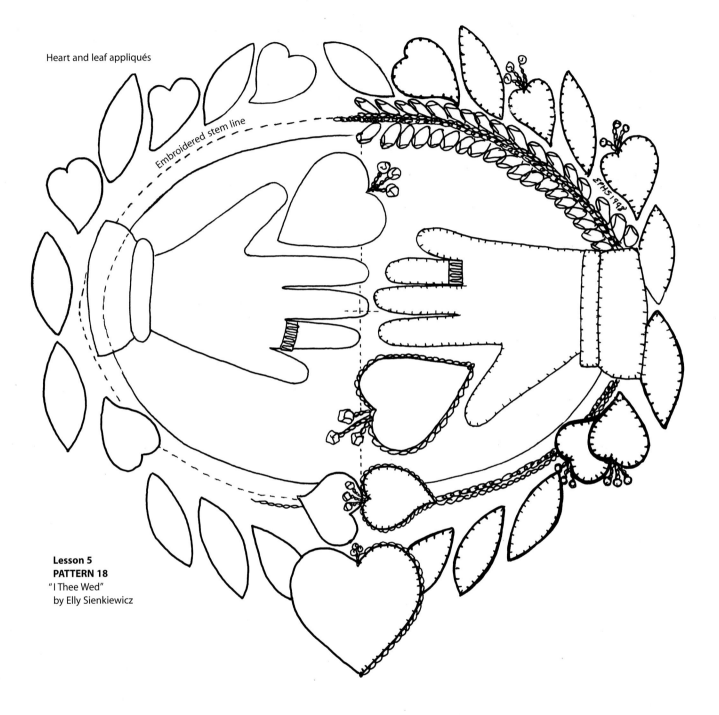

Embroidered stem line

Lesson 5
PATTERN 18
"I Thee Wed"
by Elly Sienkiewicz

Lesson 5
PATTERN 19
"Call Me Quiltmaker"
by Elly Sienkiewicz

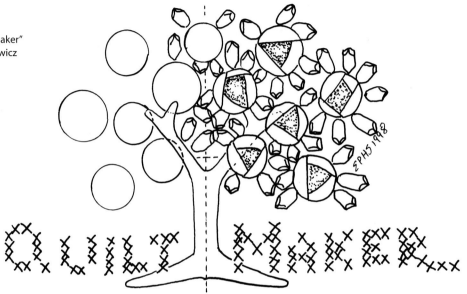

Pattern 19's Cross Stitch Alphabet Chart

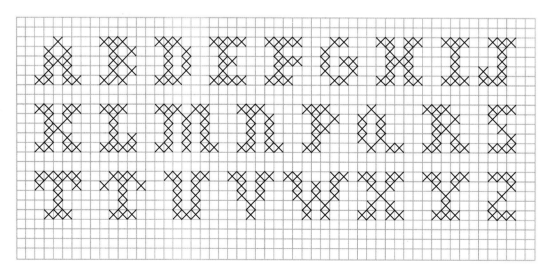

Lesson 5
PATTERN 20
"Lovey Dovey"
by Elly Sienkiewicz

Separate here to draw
shoulder line on the
UltraSuede

Lesson 5
PATTERN 21
"Thirty Years Married"
by Elly Sienkiewicz

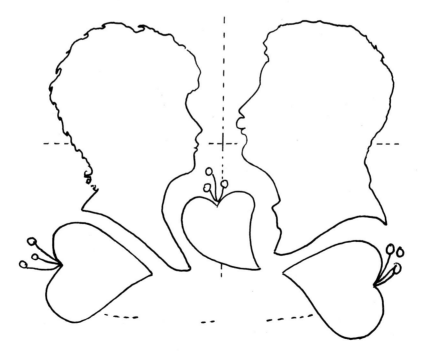

Lesson 6
PATTERN 23
"Heart Trellis with Roses"
by Laurie Toensing

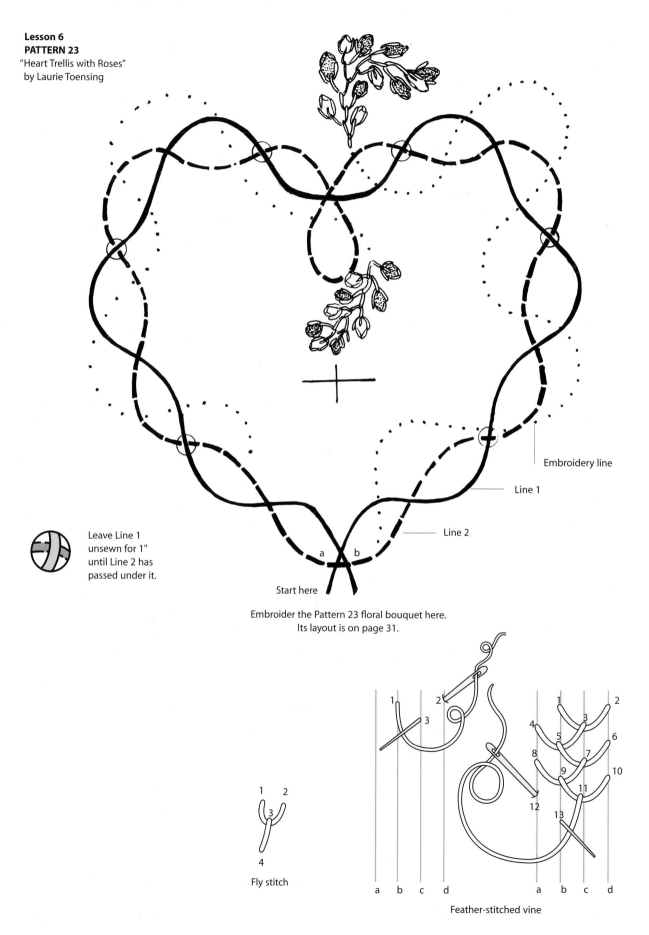

Embroidery line

Line 1

Line 2

Leave Line 1
unsewn for 1"
until Line 2 has
passed under it.

a   b

Start here

Embroider the Pattern 23 floral bouquet here.
Its layout is on page 31.

1   2
3
4

Fly stitch

Feather-stitched vine

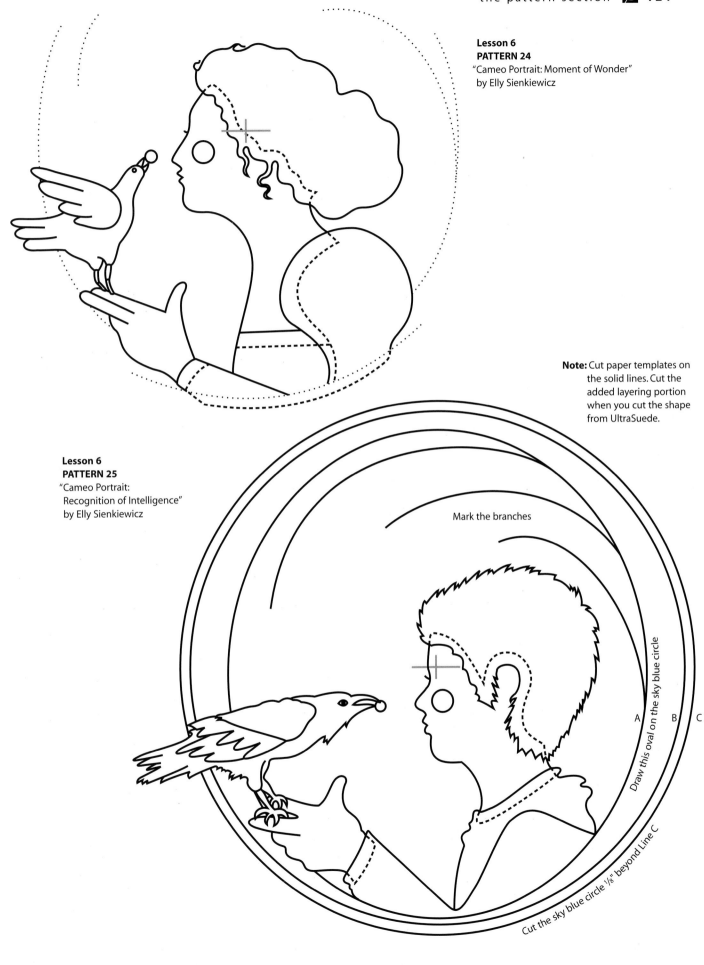

Lesson 6
PATTERN 24
"Cameo Portrait: Moment of Wonder"
by Elly Sienkiewicz

Note: Cut paper templates on the solid lines. Cut the added layering portion when you cut the shape from UltraSuede.

Lesson 6
PATTERN 25
"Cameo Portrait: Recognition of Intelligence"
by Elly Sienkiewicz

Mark the branches

Draw this oval on the sky blue circle

A   B   C

Cut the sky blue circle ⅛" beyond Line C

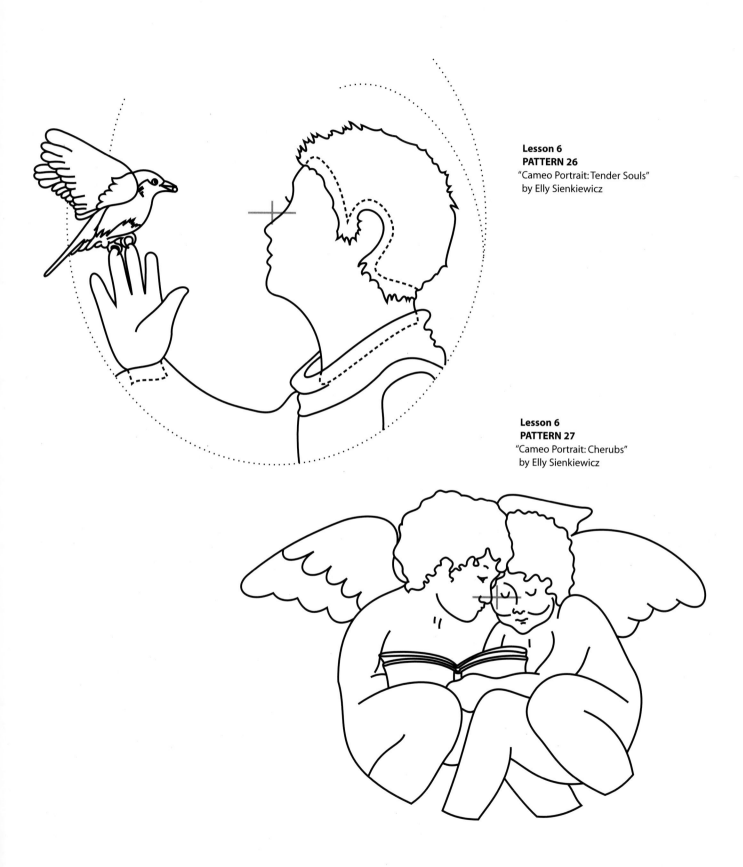

Lesson 6
PATTERN 26
"Cameo Portrait: Tender Souls"
by Elly Sienkiewicz

Lesson 6
PATTERN 27
"Cameo Portrait: Cherubs"
by Elly Sienkiewicz

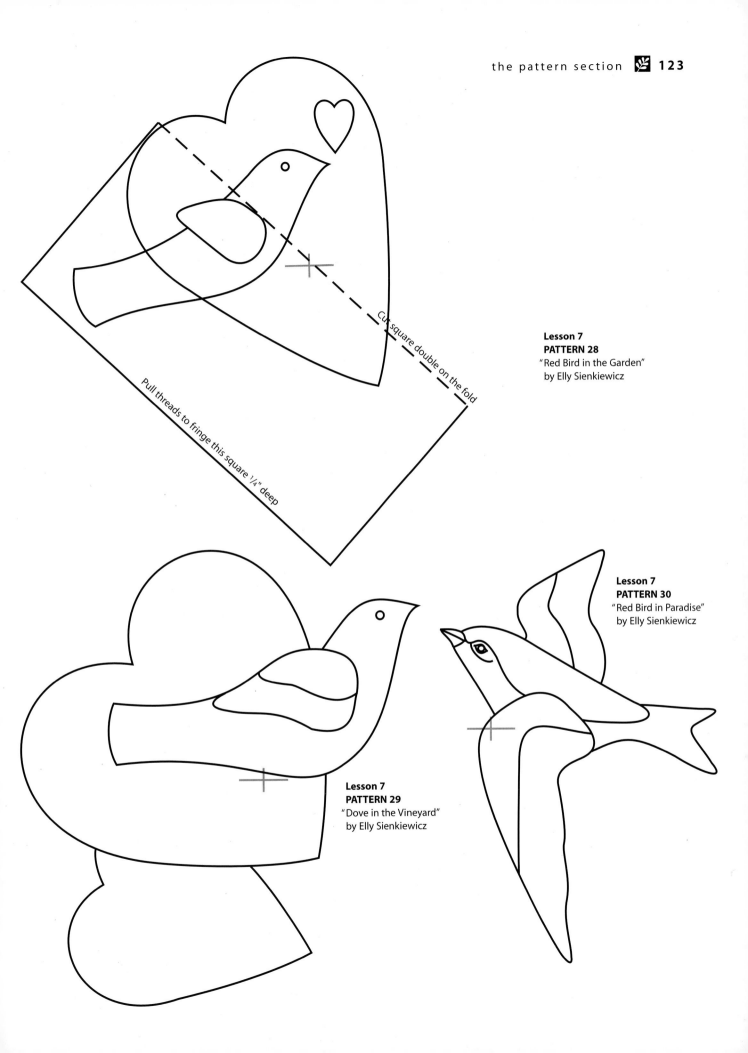

Cut square double on the fold

Pull threads to fringe this square ¹⁄₄" deep

Lesson 7
PATTERN 28
"Red Bird in the Garden"
by Elly Sienkiewicz

Lesson 7
PATTERN 30
"Red Bird in Paradise"
by Elly Sienkiewicz

Lesson 7
PATTERN 29
"Dove in the Vineyard"
by Elly Sienkiewicz

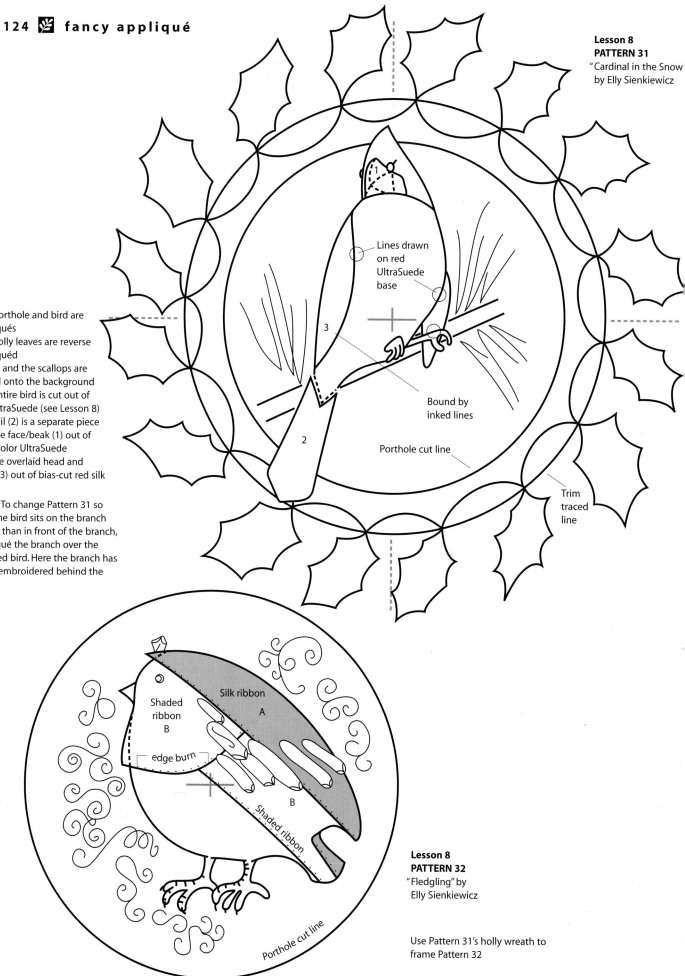

Lines drawn
on red
UltraSuede
base

Bound by
inked lines

Porthole cut line

Trim
traced
line

- The porthole and bird are appliqués
- The holly leaves are reverse appliquéd
- Line B and the scallops are traced onto the background
- The entire bird is cut out of red UltraSuede (see Lesson 8)
- The tail (2) is a separate piece
- Cut the face/beak (1) out of gold color UltraSuede
- Cut the overlaid head and body (3) out of bias-cut red silk

Note: To change Pattern 31 so that the bird sits on the branch rather than in front of the branch, appliqué the branch over the finished bird. Here the branch has been embroidered behind the bird.

Shaded
ribbon
B

Silk ribbon
A

edge burn

Shaded ribbon

B

Lesson 8
PATTERN 32
"Fledgling" by
Elly Sienkiewicz

Use Pattern 31's holly wreath to frame Pattern 32

Porthole cut line

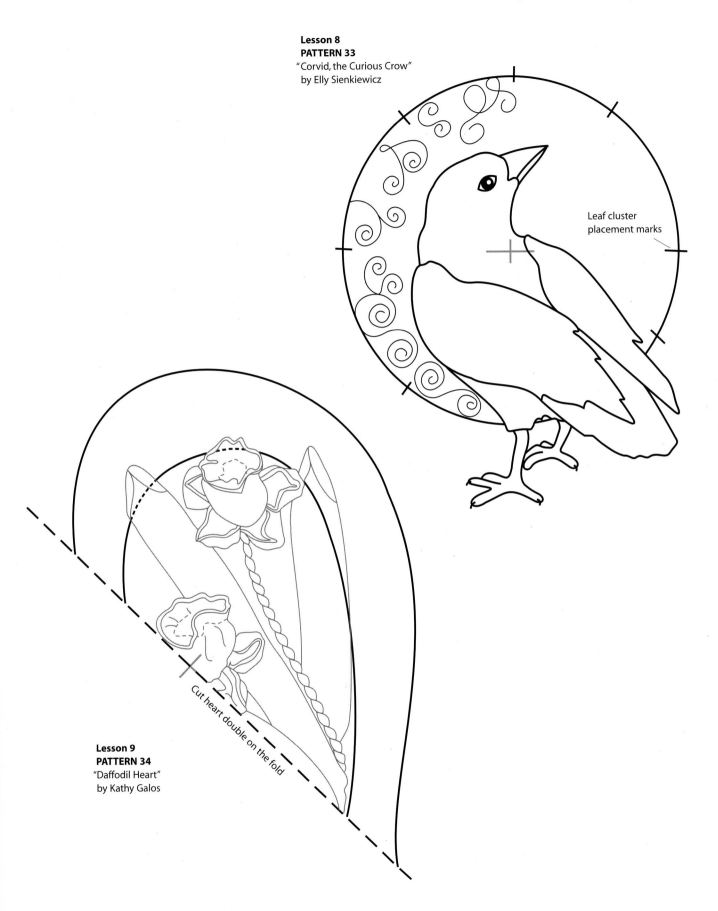

Lesson 8
PATTERN 33
"Corvid, the Curious Crow"
by Elly Sienkiewicz

Leaf cluster
placement marks

Cut heart double on the fold

Lesson 9
PATTERN 34
"Daffodil Heart"
by Kathy Galos

Lesson 9
PATTERN 35
"Messenger of Love"
by Elly Sienkiewicz

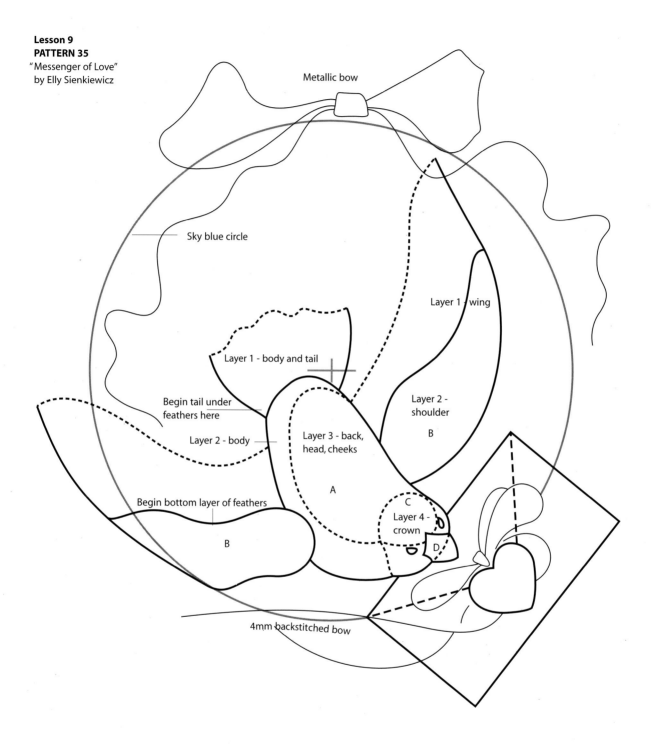

Metallic bow

Sky blue circle

Layer 1 - wing

Layer 1 - body and tail

Begin tail under
feathers here

Layer 2 -
shoulder

B

Layer 2 - body

Layer 3 - back,
head, cheeks

A

Begin bottom layer of feathers

C

Layer 4 -
crown

D

B

4mm backstitched bow

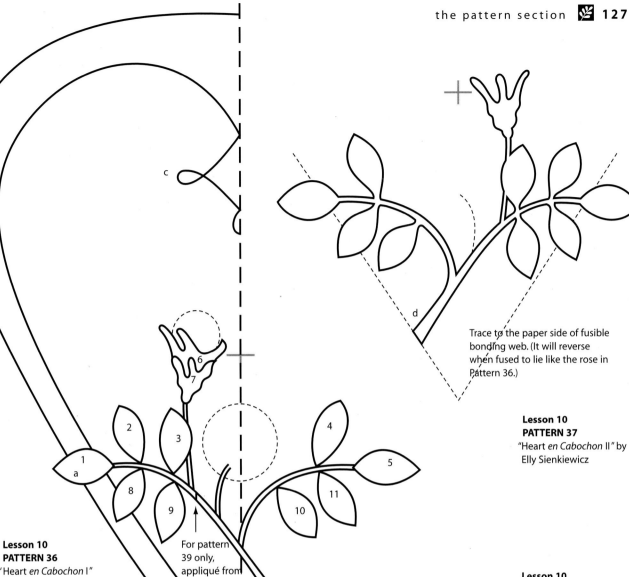

c

6
7

2 3   4

1   5

a

8   11

9   10

For pattern
39 only,
appliqué from
arrow to
base of stem

A   B   E

b

d

Trace to the paper side of fusible
bonding web. (It will reverse
when fused to lie like the rose in
Pattern 36.)

Lesson 10
PATTERN 37
"Heart *en Cabochon* II" by
Elly Sienkiewicz

Lesson 10
PATTERN 36
"Heart *en Cabochon* I"
and
Lesson 10
PATTERN 39
"Heart *en Cabochon* IV"
by Elly Sienkiewicz

Lesson 10
PATTERN 38
"Heart *en Cabochon* III"
by Elly Sienkiewicz

Note: Letters on the pattern
refer to the key and
instructions in Figure 83,
Lesson 10, page 87.

d

Lesson 11
PATTERN 40
"Trout in Pussy Willow Time"
by Elly Sienkiewicz

Lesson 11
PATTERN 41
"Lake Trout Spring"
by Elly Sienkiewicz

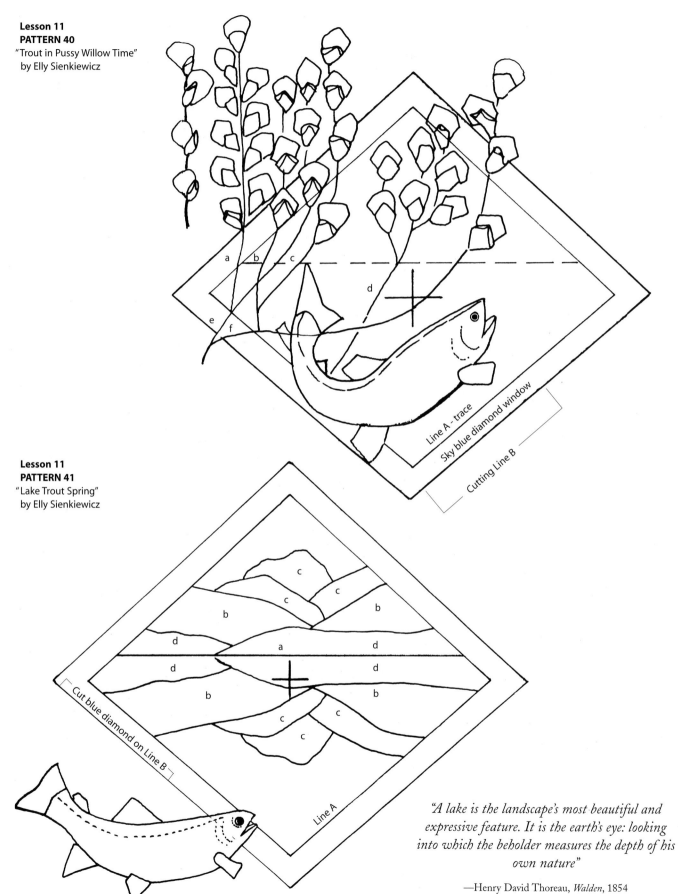

Line A - trace

Sky blue diamond window

Cutting Line B

Cut blue diamond on Line B

Line A

"A lake is the landscape's most beautiful and expressive feature. It is the earth's eye: looking into which the beholder measures the depth of his own nature"

—Henry David Thoreau, *Walden*, 1854

Lesson 11
PATTERN 42
"Blue Marlin off Patagonia"
by Elly Sienkiewicz

Lesson 12
PATTERN 43
"Time is the Stream I Go A-Fishing In"
by Elly Sienkiewicz

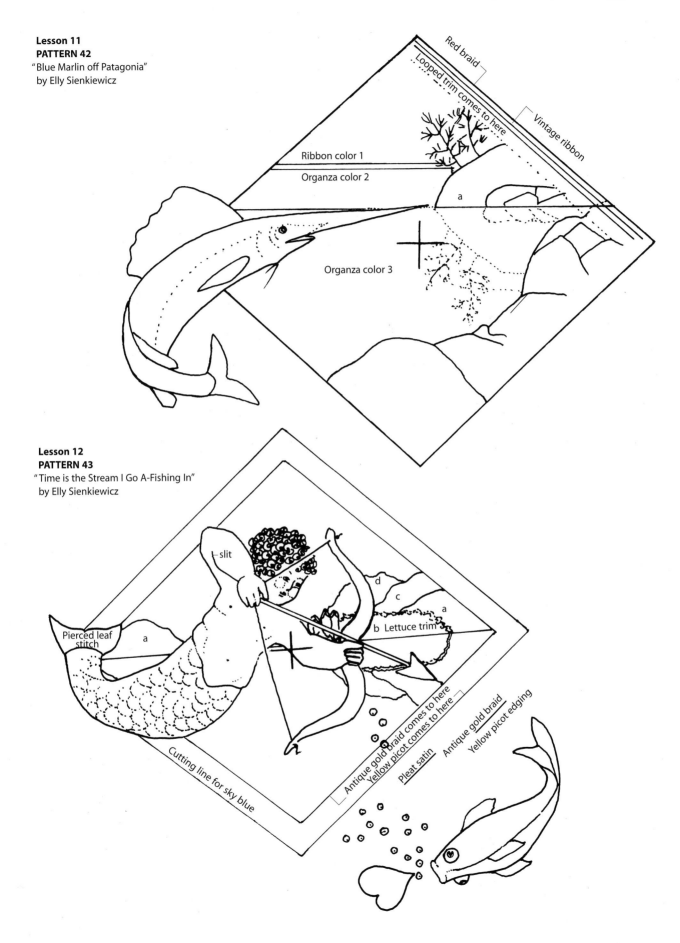

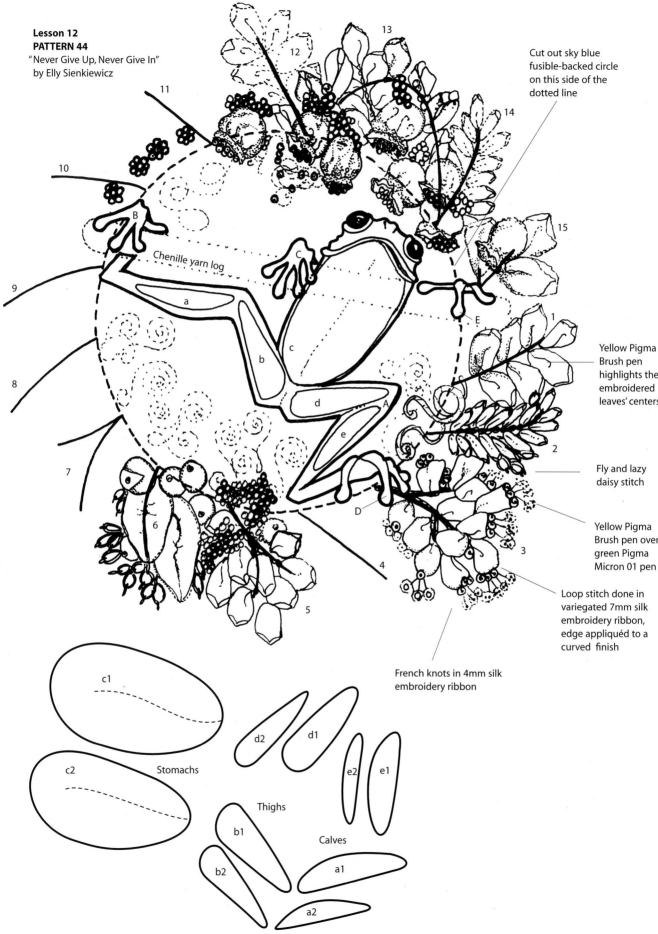

Lesson 12
PATTERN 44
"Never Give Up, Never Give In"
by Elly Sienkiewicz

Cut out sky blue fusible-backed circle on this side of the dotted line

Chenille yarn log

Yellow Pigma Brush pen highlights the embroidered leaves' centers

Fly and lazy daisy stitch

Yellow Pigma Brush pen over green Pigma Micron 01 pen

Loop stitch done in variegated 7mm silk embroidery ribbon, edge appliquéd to a curved finish

French knots in 4mm silk embroidery ribbon

Stomachs

Thighs

Calves

c1

c2

d2 d1

e2 e1

b1

b2

a1

a2

a
b
c
d
e
f
g
h
i
j
k
l
m

Key for "Grackles and Grapes"

The techniques needed to make Elly's front cover block, "Grackles and Grapes", are in Lessons 6, 7, 8, and 9. By following this key, you won't need a printed pattern to customize this spectacular block. See the block in its entirety on page 1.

(a) 16" background square of P&B Textile's Baltimore Beauties® neutral grape print (used wrong side up)

(b) Botanical print cut-out edge-fused to background (see Collage and Chintzwork, pages 69-70). P&B Textile's Baltimore Beauties® grape print in green and purple is used here

(c) Grape bunch quilted around, stuffed through slits in the background cloth, then embroidery-outlined

(d) Mokuba organdy ribbon overlay, cut out into grape bunch shape, edge-sealed with clear nail polish, and blanket stitched (page 39)

(e) Blanket stitch and tailor's buttonhole embroidery in cotton, wool, silk, and rayon flosses (page 39)

(f) Onlaid appliqué grapes of edge-sealed vintage ribbon (shaded rayon ribbon and velvet ribbon), blanket stitched (page 39) over the grapes printed on the base appliqué

(g) Crewel stitched leaf veins in one and two threads of cotton or silk embroidery floss (page 26)

(h) Overdyed chenille yarn (page 86) glue-basted (page 87) and couched into an asymmetrically entwined vine

(i) Bias-cut silk ribbon stem sewn to a circle (8 3/4" outside diameter) drawn centered on the 16" background square. Use 1"-wide Artemis bias-cut silk ribbon in Earthmother and Stem Method 2, page 60

(j) Backyard birds: Choose mated birds from a full color bird guide. Photocopy the illustration's models to desired size. Make templates from their outlines. Construct each bird using techniques for stumpwork birds described in Lesson 7. Use a magnifier to spot the lessons' details in the birds on the cover of *Fancy Appliqué*.
Elly began the female grackle (on the left) by covering a stumpwork-style padded base with Offray's size 9 Spectrum Brown shaded wired ribbon. The male grackle began with a 2"-wide (50mm) black taffeta-like ribbon overlaid with iridescent looking Mokuba organdy ribbon in shades of blue to black. The same effect could be achieved by covering the stumpwork padded base with a black UltraSuede body shape basted under a layer of Mokuba Shaded Organdy ribbon #4881SK, color #5, 50mm wide. Cut the basted ribbon a little larger than the UltraSuede and edge-seal the ribbon's edges with clear nail polish. Needleturn both layers over the bird's padding. The simplest approach to a fancywork bird is to follow the procedure for making the crow taught on pages 80-81. The 4mm and 7mm feathers are hand-dyed silk embroidery ribbon from Petals and The Thread Gatherer

(k) Thai silk dupioni hearts, edge-sealed, needleturned, top-stitched, and edge-embroidered in crewel stitch (page 86)

(l) Legs/feet drawn in black Pigma Micron 01 and further embellished with stitching in brownish YLI Silk 100 sewing thread

(m) Freehand inscription in black Pigma Micron 01 pen using the Copperplate Hand (page 88) over a masking taped straight-edge

Rewards Along the Way

We quiltmakers are each so different and yet feel such kinship with one another. We work stuff, goods, to make objects of tangible beauty. Even without tangible reward, this beauty affirms us. Every step of the way, when a quilt's unit finishes to our satisfaction, its beauty rewards us. This is particularly true in the Fancy Sampler genre where each block is unique, each involves some technique or artistry previously untried. A finite 12 lessons belies the magnitude of learning involved. On the one hand, a magnificent quilt, we each believe, will come from this path we follow, but could we not reward accomplishment along the way? To do so would season the journey!

Quilt shows reward the finished product: completion. Like all exhibitions, they display communal progress. For needlewomen, this tradition is venerable. It can fuel a wholesome desire to excel. Both the 19th and 20th centuries saw great American quilt shows. Annual fair catalogs from the Maryland Institute for the Promotion of the Mechanic Arts note that Album quilts hung in Baltimore, beginning in 1848 and prizes were given. This venue surely encouraged the Baltimore Album Quilt Style's rapid rise to excellence. So significant was the Centennial Exhibition in Philadelphia in 1876 that the Smithsonian's Arts and Industries Museum displayed much of it for the 1976 bicentennial. It, too, featured the glories of needlework. Within our own lifetimes we have seen 20th century quilt shows achieve international acclaim with prize money worthy of fine art masterpieces.

Such exhibitions foster wholesome competition and thread our quiltmaking tradition from one century to the next. On the one hand, elitism is criticized by those wishing to reassure mid-level performance. On the other hand, we all share the excitement and even the reflected glory when someone excels at an art we admire. The world would be a dull place with no best and brightest or no freedom to strive for betterment. Yet some of us dislike competitions, and each knows reward need not come from a public forum. Joy comes when our own work surprises us; when you attain a level you had not realized you could reach. In the spirit then of private pleasure, of setting your sights high and stretching to reach them, the certificates of mastery are provided on the next few pages. Use them to record setting an honorable goal and attaining it. Add their tangible reward to your quilt's history or simply acknowledge that you've scaled that mountain and are ready to attempt the next. I feel sure you will rise beautifully to these challenges and in that faith, add my signature to your certificate. I'm privileged to be able to join you this way. Thank you for making me a part of your appliqué journey.

Elly Sienkiewicz

Certificate of Achievement

This degree,
a Bachelor of Arts in Appliqué,
Honoris Causa,

is presented to

....

In Recognition of Exceptional
Needlework Performance
through Studies in Fancy Appliqué

Given at _____

On this _____ day of ____ in the year _____

Signature _____

Elly Sienkiewicz

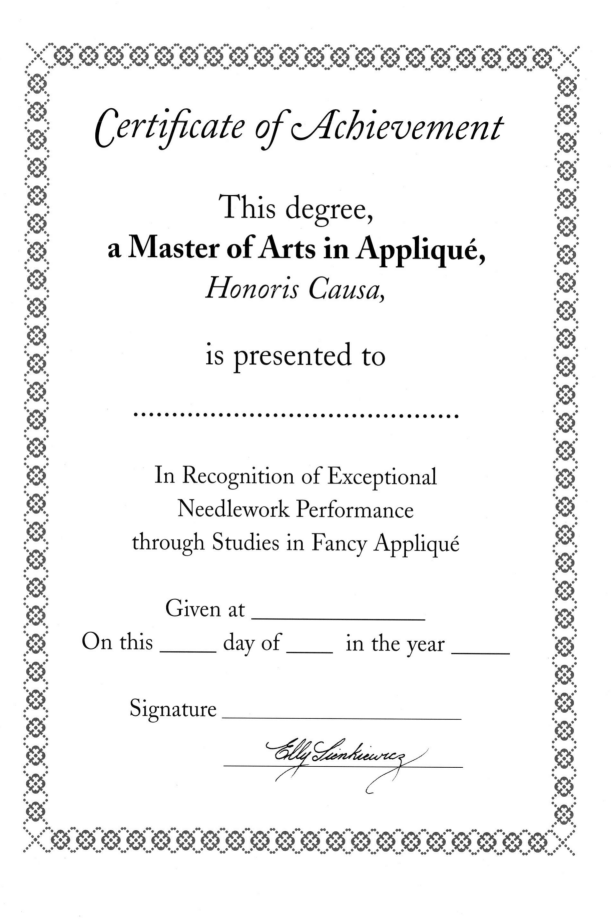

Certificate of Achievement

This degree,
a Master of Arts in Appliqué,
Honoris Causa,

is presented to

....

In Recognition of Exceptional
Needlework Performance
through Studies in Fancy Appliqué

Given at _____

On this _____ day of _____ in the year _____

Signature _____

Certificate of Achievement

This degree,
a Doctor of Philosophy in Appliqué,
Honoris Causa,

is presented to

....

In Recognition of Exceptional
Needlework Performance
through Studies in Fancy Appliqué

Given at _____

On this _____ day of _____ in the year _____

Signature _____

Elly Sienkiewicz

Part IV: Appendix

Quilt Specifications and Sets

The sets of Fancy Sampler Quilts I and II were designed by Lisa McCulley, who also assembled, machine quilted, and finished them. Fancy Sampler Quilt I's quilting pattern was designed by Susan Connolly Clark. These original quilts require advanced quiltmaking skills. To aid you here, the designer shares each quilt's set diagram, yardage requirements, and cutting instructions.

Fancy Sampler Quilt I

Blocks by 1997 Appliqué Academy Challenge entrants and Elly Sienkiewicz; quilt designed, pieced, and quilted by Lisa D. McCulley; quilting design by Susan L. Connolly Clark, 54½" x 54½", 1997-1998.

FABRIC REQUIREMENTS

1¼ yards for background of appliqué blocks
⅜ yard light fabric for triangles circling the octagon and the pieced feather strips. Purchase ⅝ yard more if you choose to add a narrow accent strip around the blocks and quilt as Lisa did.
⅜ yard of dark fabric for the pieced feather strips and diamond tips
⅜ yard for kite shapes of star arms
2½ yards for inner diamond border and outer border
3½ yards for backing
½ yard for (2¼" cut width) binding

CUTTING INSTRUCTIONS

- **Background Squares for Appliqué Blocks:** To make twenty-eight 6½" finished blocks and one 7¼" finished octagon, cut one strip 7¾" wide and four strips 7" wide. Cut one octagon from the 7¾"–wide strip, then trim the strip to 7" wide and cut four 7" squares. Cut the remaining twenty-four 7" squares from the four 7"-wide strips.
- **Alternative:** Make twenty-nine 6½" finished blocks and add small strips of fabric to each edge of the octagon shape to make it 7¾" unfinished.
- **Inner Triangles Circling Octagon:** Cut four 3" squares, cut in half diagonally to yield eight half-square triangles.

- **Kite Shapes for Star Arms:** From template plastic make a template for the "kite" shape: draw two lines perpendicular (an "L" shape), one measuring 2⅛" long, the other measuring 5" long. Trace onto tracing paper, flip the tracing paper and match the points to create the kite shape. Redraw onto template plastic and add ¼" seam allowances. To make eight kite shapes, cut two 4½"-wide strips, then lay template to fabric and cut eight kite shapes.
- **Pieced Feather Strips:** Cut thirty-six 1⅞" squares from two 1⅞"-wide strips of dark fabric, then cut diagonally to yield 72 half-square triangles. Cut forty-four 1⅞" squares from two 1⅞"-wide strips of light fabric, then cut diagonally to yield 88 half-square triangles.
- **Diamond Tips:** Cut two 1½"-wide strips of dark fabric, cut a 45° angle, place 1½" line of ruler on the 45° cut line and cut a second 45° angle. Cut 8 diamonds total.
- **Diamonds for Inner Border:** Cut six 5"-wide strips, cut a 45° angle, place 5" line of ruler on the 45° cut line, and cut a second 45° angle. Make 24 diamonds total.

• *Outer Border:* For the eight border pieces, cut eight 6"-wide strips. (Depending on the actual width of the fabric you may only get one border piece from each strip.) Cut the left end of four strips at a 45° angle, and cut the right end of the other four strips at a 45° angle. The other ends of the strips will be a mitered corners. Four center setting triangles are needed to complete the outside border: cut one 10½" square, then cut it diagonally in both directions to yield 4 quarter-square triangles.

Fancy Sampler Quilt II

Blocks by Elly Sienkiewicz; quilt designed, pieced, and quilted by Lisa D. McCulley, 65½" x 65½", 1998

FABRIC REQUIREMENTS:
1¼ yards total (¼ yard white-on-white, ¼ yard dark beige, ¾ yard light beige) for background of appliqué blocks
¾ yard green fabric for framing triangles and corner border triangles
1¼ yards very light beige, 1¼ yards medium-light beige fabric for setting trapezoids for corner border triangles
½ yard dark beige fabric for inner border
2 yards medium-light beige fabric for outer border
4 yards for backing
½ yard for (1½" cut width) binding

CUTTING INSTRUCTIONS
• *Background Squares for Appliqué Blocks:* To make twenty-one 7½" finished blocks, cut five 8" squares from one 8"-wide white-on-white strip, then cut four 8" squares from one 8"-wide dark beige strip, and twelve 8" squares from three 8"-wide light beige strips.
• *Green Framing Triangles:* Cut forty-two 3⅜" squares from three 3⅜"-wide strips, then cut each square diagonally to yield 84 half-square triangles to set around each block.
• *Setting Trapezoids:* Cut twenty-one 7" squares from five 7" very light beige strips, and twenty-one 7" squares from five 7" medium-light beige strips. Cut each square diagonally in both directions to yield 168 quarter-square triangles. Measuring from the longest edge of the triangle toward the point, cut a trapezoid 2⅛" tall.
• *Corner Border Triangles:* Cut two 8½" squares from green fabric. Cut each square diagonally to yield 4 half-square triangles.
• *Inner Border:* Cut four 3"-wide strips. Cut the strips in half to yield eight pieces for the inner border. Cut two 5" squares, then cut each diagonally to yield four half-square triangles for the center setting triangle.
• *Outer Border:* Cut eight 8"-wide strips. You'll get one border piece from each strip and will have enough to cut four trapezoids for the pieces to complete the center setting triangles.

Classes

Fancy Appliqué introduces you to the "Fancy Sampler Quilt," a trove for shop classes and block-of-the-month kits. The following course descriptions use *Fancy Appliqué* as a text and may be used verbatim. For each, the skill level is "All," and a copy of *Fancy Appliqué* is needed in class. Basic sewing supplies (page 12) and the materials listed for each pattern provide the class supply list.

Half-day Classes

1. **Go 100% Fancy (100% Cotton + *Fancy Appliqué*)**
Learn reverse and onlaid appliqué by visible running stitch needleturn to reveal a pieced background. Finesse Fraktur and Cloissonné appliqué to burst your "Fancy Sampler Quilt" into bloom! (Patterns 1 & 2, Lesson 1, *Fancy Appliqué*.)

2. **Fancy Twist 'n Fancy Twine**
Appliqué a Sampler Quilt heart block with pretzel twists, variegated cotton dimension, and needleturn challenges (points, twines, curves, and corners). Adorn your hearts to the hilt with a bouquet of silk ribbon-embroidered rose and wisteria and a beaded ribbon tie. (Pattern 3, Lesson 1, *Fancy Appliqué*)

3. **Appliqué, Reversed: Open to Ribbon and Romance!**
Perfect reverse appliqué: Fill three Fancy Sampler Quilt hearts with 1) ribbon collage; 2) bead and thread embroidery; 3) heat-transferred ink engraving and silk ribbon fancywork. (Patterns 5, 7, & 8; Lesson 2, *Fancy Appliqué*)

One Day (or Two Half-day) Classes

4. **"I Thee Wed": The Oval Wreaths of Fancy Sampler Quilt II**
Learn a wealth of fancywork! Create a folk-inspired wreath with UltraSuede appliqué, crewel-stitched stems, silk ribbon leaves, goldwork embroidered embellishment, copperplate ink inscription, and ribbon overlay. (*Fancy Appliqué*'s Pattern 18 will quick-start your Fancy Sampler Quilt II.)

5. **"Lovey Dovey": The Mixed Media Birds of *Fancy Appliqué***
Create an oval wreath of crewel-stitched goldwork, silk ribbon, and UltraSuede. Fashion layered UltraSuede doves, silk-winged and tinged with colored pencil and ink. (*Fancy Appliqué*'s Pattern 20 gives wings to your *Fancy Appliqué* Fancy Sampler Quilt II.)

6. **Fancy Is as Fancy Does**
Learn the joy of *Fancy Appliqué*'s Pattern 24: couch a herringbone wreath, crewel stitch fruit boughs in variegated silk ribbon, then UltraSuede appliqué (and silk-feather) the dove and maiden in Elly's "Moment of Wonder."

7. **Laurie's Tri-twined Wreath**
Weave ⅛"-wide bias-cut cloth! Embroider the stunningly simple bower with a pearl cotton fly stitch vine of silk ribbon foliage and flowers. Master this gem (Pattern 23, *Fancy Appliqué*) with fine milliners needle and silk thread appliqué.

8. **Crow in Bittersweet by Mixed Media Appliqué**
Sculpt a realistic crow wreathed by dimensional foliage. Study the artistry of silk ribbon embroidery, goldwork, vintage trims, UltraSuede, Stumpwork Appliqué, pen, ink, pencil, shaded wired ribbon, and bead embroidery. (Pattern 33, *Fancy Appliqué*.)

Two-day Classes

9. **Stumpwork Appliqué: A Silk Dove, Wreathed in Hydrangea**

   Recreate a Victorian postcard image for your Fancy Sampler Quilt. Stitch a romantic dove in dimensional silk stumpwork appliqué on cotton. Learn ribbon embroidery, goldwork, ink, and colored pencil shading. This block is sculptural, painterly, and challenging! (Pattern 35, *Fancy Appliqué*.)

10. **A Master's Degree in Appliqué, for Honorary Causes**

    Work *Fancy Appliqué*'s Patterns 36, 37, 38, and 39: Couch their herringbone and vintage trim heart wreaths. Within each wreath stitch a miniature rose, thereby reviewing appliqué's finest challenges. *Fancy Appliqué* suggests that making these blocks is worth an M.S.A!

11. **Diamond-Framed Fancy Miniature Scenes**

    Learn *Fancy Appliqué*'s Patterns 40, 41, and 43. Organdy ribbon casts watery reflections of silk landscapes, edge-burned. Mixed media fish and even a stumpwork appliquéd merman (Ultra-Suede and vintage ribbon) inhabit these vignettes framed in fancywork. Your Fancy Sampler Quilt needs a scenery block !

12. **"Never Give Up", a Ph.D. in Appliqué, *Honoris Causa***

    The feisty frog block of *Fancy Appliqué*'s Pattern 44 teaches multi-layer stumpwork UltraSuede appliqué; chenille and goldwork; bead, silk, and organdy embroidery; dimensional ribbon flowers; pen and colored pencil shading. This is appliqué as fancy as it gets!

Sources

Teaching and Lecturing: Elly Sienkiewicz, 5540 30th Street, NW, Washington, DC 20015 (FAX (202) 537-2995). While it is best to schedule far in advance, same year scheduling occasionally works. Please write for teaching prospectus.

Elly Sienkiewicz's Appliqué Academy: A memorable bi-annual Quilt Retreat! For brochure (mails late summer) send a large self-addressed envelope (two first class stamps) to: Bette Augustine, Director, PO Box 13197, Hayward, WI 54843; Phone (715) 462-9030; FAX (715) 462-4077 email: bette@win.bright.net. http://www.ellysienkiewicz.com

Kits for Making *Fancy Appliqué*'s Lesson Block of the Month: Send a SASE for information to Summer House Needleworks, 6375 Oley Turnpike Road, Oley, PA 19547. (610) 689-9090; FAX (610) 689-8020. Summer House is *Fancy Appliqué*'s fabric, ribbon, and trim treasure trove. It is also a source for virtually the entire Caron Collection of overdyed cotton, silk, and wool embroidery threads, plus YLI and Tire Silk sewing thread.

Trims, Ribbon, Chenille, Needles, Thread, and ⅛" Bias Bars by Heirloom Stitches: Quilter's Resource, Box 148850, Chicago, IL. **Wholesale to the trade**: cite *Fancy Appliqué*'s page and pattern.

Artemis Bias-Cut Silk Ribbon: All the widths and colors used in *Fancy Appliqué*. Send SASE to Artemis, Diana Dickey, 179 High Street, South Portland, ME 04106. (207) 741-2497; Fax: (207) 741-2497.

Trims (both Vintage and Modern): Lacis, 3163 Adeline Avenue, Berkeley, CA 94705. (510) 843-5018. Also Sandy's Notions, 7417 N. Knoxville, Peoria, IL 61614. (309) 689-1943; Fax: (309) 689-1942. **Wholesale to the trade:** *Fancy Appliqué* uses trims #7532, #2074, #7232, #739, #233-833, and T41.

All the Hard-to-find Ribbons for *Fancy Appliqué*: French shaded wire edged ribbons, velvet, spark organdy (for overlays) and gold-edged spark organdy. Wholesale with actual samples to the trade only: Creative Import Design, 10 Belgrade Ave., Youngstown, OH 44505.1-888-8 RIBBON.

Mokuba Ribbon named in *Fancy Appliqué*: MKB/Mokuba Ribbon: (212) 302-5010. Ask for Linda Chernick. email: MKBLady@aol.com http://www.festivegiftwrap.com

Two exceptional sources for hand-dyed silk ribbons are: Jenifer Buechel, Box 118, Mountainview Drive, West Mifflin, PA 15122; and **The Thread Gatherer**, 2108 Norcrest Drive, Boise, ID 83705. Send a SASE for information.

UltraSuede: G-Street Fabrics (Mail Order: $10.00 for samples. 11854 Rockville Pike, Rockville, MD 20852. Charge card orders: (800) 333-9191.

One-stop Shop: The Cotton Patch, 1025 Brown Avenue, Lafayette, CA, 94549 (800) 835-4418. Mail order for materials needed to do the blocks in *Fancy Appliqué*. Carries P&B Textiles' *Baltimore Beauties*® fabric and the ribbon, trims, thread, and notions you'll need. Sells *Appliqué 12 Easy Ways!*, *Romancing Ribbons into Flowers*, *Appliqué Paper Greetings*, and all other books in print by Elly Sienkiewicz. Excellent international service.

Index

About the Author

Eleanor Hamilton Sienkiewicz has written fourteen acclaimed needlework books; her impact on the late 20th century quilt revival is indelible. She has been welcomed on six continents as author, teacher, and lecturer. Her voice is intelligent, her persona empathetic, and her needlework exquisite.

Sienkiewicz's published pieces appeal to both craft and scholarly interests, but her most loyal readers are quiltmakers interested in appliqué. For 17 years, Elly has honed her expertise on the Baltimore Album Quilt style of the mid-19th century. These quilts have become for Elly and thousands like her, "the fascinating ladies of bygone Baltimore." The question of why these quilts have such broad and intense appeal is one she addresses in *Spoken Without a Word* and in her nine volume *Baltimore Beauties and Beyond* book series.

Hand appliqué, fancywork, and the Victorian Album Quilt genre itself have gained increasing prominence during Elly's author years. This quilt genre's appeal to art and antique collectors and investors is the stuff of headlines. (By the mid 1990s a vintage quilt dubbed "The NY Album" by the Kopfs of America Hurrah! Antiques had fetched $264,000 at a NYC auction.) The Album Quilt style—a collection of blocks on a theme—is in full revival. The Fancy Sampler Quilt is the 20th century's contribution to this artistic movement. It provides the stitcher with an heirloom canvas for her art, an Album in which to record her needlework journey. Albums are the perfect quilt form (and communal forum) for navigating our way into a new millennium. This affirmation of old loves—history, religion, and art—in the fellowship of quiltmakers is, author Sienkiewicz notes, a source of serenity for many. And her own happiness, students note, is contagious. A teacher by nature, Elly was educated at Wellesley College and received a master's degree from the University of Pennsylvania. She devoted seven years to teaching secondary school history and social studies before raising her children, Donald, Alex, and Katya. As a stay-at-home mom, entrepreneurial activities (including Cabin Fever Calicoes' Quiltshop by Mail) brought Mrs. Sienkiewicz increasing prominence in the burgeoning quilt industry. She continues to live in Washington, DC, with her husband of 30 years, Stan Sienkiewicz.

Fourteen books by Elly Sienkiewicz:

Fancy Appliqué —1999
Baltimore Album Legacy —1998
Appliqué Paper Greetings! —1997
Romancing Ribbons into Flowers — 1996
Papercuts and Plenty, Baltimore Beauties and Beyond, Vol. III —1995
Baltimore Album Revival —1994
Appliqué 12 Borders and Medallions —1994
Dimensional Appliqué —1993
Design a Baltimore Album Quilt —1992
Appliqué 12 Easy Ways! —1991
Baltimore Beauties and Beyond, Vol. II —1992
Baltimore Album Quilts —1990
Baltimore Beauties and Beyond, Vol. I —1989
Spoken Without a Word —1983

Other Fine Books From C&T Publishing:

An Amish Adventure: 2nd Edition, Roberta Horton

Art & Inspirations: Ruth B. McDowell, Ruth B. McDowell

The Art of Silk Ribbon Embroidery, Judith Baker Montano

The Artful Ribbon, Candace Kling

Color From the Heart: Seven Great Ways to Make Quilts with Colors You Love, Gai Perry

Crazy Quilt Handbook, Judith Montano

Designing the Doll: From Concept to Construction, Susanna Oroyan

Easy Pieces: Creative Color Play with Two Simple Blocks, Margaret J. Miller

Elegant Stitches: Judith Baker Montano

Enduring Grace: Quilts from the Shelburne Museum Collection, Celia Y. Oliver

Everything Flowers: Quilts from the Garden, Jean and Valori Wells

Exploring Machine Trapunto: New Dimensions, Hari Walner

The Fabric Makes the Quilt, Roberta Horton

Forever Yours, Wedding Quilts, Clothing & Keepsakes, Amy Barickman

Freddy's House: Brilliant Color in Quilts, Freddy Moran

Free Stuff for Crafty Kids on the Internet, Judy Heim and Gloria Hansen

Free Stuff for Quilters on the Internet, 2nd Ed. Judy Heim and Gloria Hansen

Free Stuff for Sewing Fanatics on the Internet, Judy Heim and Gloria Hansen

Free Stuff for Stitchers on the Internet, Judy Heim and Gloria Hansen

Hand Quilting with Alex Anderson: Six Projects for Hand Quilters, Alex Anderson

Heirloom Machine Quilting, Third Edition, Harriet Hargrave

Impressionist Quilts, Gai Perry

Jacobean Rhapsodies: Composing with 28 Appliqué Designs, Patricia B. Campbell and Mimi Ayars

Judith Baker Montano: Art & Inspirations, Judith Baker Montano

Kaleidoscopes : Wonders of Wonder, Cozy Baker

Mastering Machine Appliqué, Harriet Hargrave

Mastering Quilt Marking, Pepper Cory

The New England Quilt Museum Quilts: Featuring the Story of the Mill Girls. With Instructions for 5 Heirloom Quilts, Jennifer Gilbert

The New Sampler Quilt, Diana Leone

Patchwork Quilts Made Easy, Jean Wells (co-published with Rodale Press, Inc.)

The Photo Transfer Handbook: Snap It, Print It, Stitch It!, Jean Ray Laury

Pieced Clothing Variations, Yvonne Porcella

Piecing: Expanding the Basics, Ruth B. McDowell

Quilts for Fabric Lovers, Alex Anderson

Quilts from the Civil War: Nine Projects, Historical Notes, Diary Entries, Barbara Brackman

Quilts, Quilts, and More Quilts! Diana McClun and Laura Nownes

Rotary Cutting with Alex Anderson: Tips, Techniques, and Projects, Alex Anderson

Say It with Quilts, Diana McClun and Laura Nownes

Scrap Quilts: The Art of Making Do, Roberta Horton

Six Color World: Color, Cloth, Quilts & Wearables, Yvonne Porcella

Skydyes: A Visual Guide to Fabric Painting, Mickey Lawler

Start Quilting with Alex Anderson: Six Projects for First-Time Quilters, Alex Anderson

Through the Garden Gate: Quilters and Their Gardens, Jean & Valori Wells

Travels with Peaky and Spike: Doreen Speckmann's Quilting Adventures, Doreen Speckmann

Wildflowers: Designs for Appliqué & Quilting, Carol Armstrong

Women of Taste: A Collaboration Celebrating Quilt Artists and Chefs, Girls, Inc.

Yvonne Porcella: Art & Inspirations, Yvonne Porcella

For more information write for a free catalog:
C&T Publishing, Inc.
P.O. Box 1456
Lafayette, CA 94549
(800) 284-1114
http://www.ctpub.com
email: ctinfo@ctpub.com

For quilting supplies:
Cotton Patch Mail Order
3405 Hall Lane, Dept. CTB
Lafayette, CA 94549
email: quiltusa@yahoo.com
(800) 835-4418
(925) 283-7883